CONFESSIONS OF A DICE DEALER

In Loving Memory of Dorell Hanson MCMLXXII / MMVIII Magna
Britannia mihi patria est MMIX et MMXVI per aspera ad triumphum

-INDEX-

-Preface-

Windmill was born in Birmingham England in 1966; he worked for various casino corporations on land in: the United Kingdom, South Africa, the United States of America and, the Bahamas. He also worked at Sea for: Atlantic Associates, The Tiber Group, Premier Cruise Lines, Royal Cruise Lines, Norwegian Cruise Lines, Greater Atlantic and Royal Caribbean.

Many thanks to all the casino crews around the world for giving me inspiration to write this book, also a special mention goes out to all our brothers and sisters whom have sadly passed away.

This book is not just about the wild days of casinos, and I send my sincere thanks to all the people I had the pleasure of meeting along the way.

Note*

This second edition is a heavily edited version correcting mistakes and, cutting out many negative aspects of the story. I have rewritten some chapters completely and reorganized others.

Windmill 2016

THE NEIGHBOURS

Throughout the late seventies and mid eighties, Great Britain was experiencing some tough economic times. The country was in turmoil, high unemployment and social unrest prevailed in many of the country's cities; including mine, Birmingham. After leaving school during the early stages of the era, things were indeed very uncertain. This story begins in one of those suburbs of Birmingham, Handsworth in 1985.

The autumn of 1985 was pretty much uneventful until the riots once again erupted in the Handsworth district of the City of Birmingham. Across the country disenfranchised youth were kicking off and the inhabitants of Handsworth decided they too wanted a piece of the action. Those involved were mostly second or third generation West Indians; infuriated by constant harassment by the local police and a distinct lack of employment opportunities in the concrete jungle.

My best mates old man used to own a boozer in Handsworth called the 'Old Gate Inn' down on Booth St; a quiet little pub down by the railway bridge which carried the then disused Snow Hill line into the nearby city. The back streets of the suburb had seen better days, most of the businesses associated with the infamous industrial revolution had long gone. Graffiti now donned the boarded up houses with burnt out cars sporadically lining the streets, all paying testimony to the deprivation of the area and adding to the gloom of an era. The riots taking place further down in Handsworth had indeed intensified on the second night, so me and my mate Nobby decided to go down and have a look at all the commotion. We managed to make it as far as the legendary 'Monte Carlo' club on the Soho Road, and here we witnessed a huge gang of geezers throwing all sorts of missiles at the coppers: bottles, bricks, shit, and anything else that could be used as a weapon. By now the coppers had had enough and they suddenly made a line across the road. The atmosphere had become very intimidating with the mob baying for their blood, when suddenly the police charged with their batons drawn looking to cave some heads in. Everybody turned around and scarpered down the road in panic. During the confusion, Nobby and me were caught up in the escalating mêlée, so we decided to leg it from the long arms of the law with the rest of the mob. Suddenly more coppers appeared in front of us, "It's a fucking ambush!" shouted some bloke as the police lines ahead opened up and police vans came rushing forward with their sirens blaring. The vans screeched to a halt and scores of coppers jumped out screaming and shouting whilst swinging their truncheons around clattering anybody on the bonce who was in range. Instinctively, we jumped into a shops doorway to hide from view. After a few seconds we peaked out of our hidey hole to watch loads of blokes with bloodied heads being thrown into the backs of the vans, some of the poor fuckers were unconscious too. "Fucking hell," said Nobby, "the snidey bastards have unmarked vans!" It was now obvious what the police were doing, the fuckers had planned it all along. They'd got the uniformed lot to charge the mob into their mates waiting down the road. "We'd better get the fuck out of here sharpish, or we'll be in A&E in half an hour and Victoria Law Courts' in the morning!" I replied. Nobby agreed and with some quick footed manoeuvring we managed to avoid the fuckers and steamed into the 'Bee Hive' pub on Soho Hill. Closing the door behind the pandemonium brought us a brief respite, however, this was not going to last for long.

"Are you 18? If you have no identification you will have to leave lads," shouted a geezer behind the bar. Everybody in the pub stopped what they were doing and glared at us. Nobby pipped up: "Mate, we are 18, and we ain't going back out there! The coppers are looking to give someone a right good kicking and it ain't gonna be us!" The bloke behind the bar shook his head, threw is towel on the bar and made his way around it to confront us. He was a big fucker too and looked like he'd been in a fair few punch ups in his time. "Listen lads, you're only in here because its all kicked off outside. We don't want any fuckin police in here...you get me? Anyway, you're not locals in this pub. I have been here for 10yrs and have never seen either of you in this boozer before. No ID means no service...now fuck off," he growled. "Oh nice one mate, cheers, looks like you want us to get nicked, and by the way, my old man runs the Old Gate!" retorted Nobby. The bloke didn't flinch, he just lifted his huge paw like hand and pointed to the door. "I think we'd better take our chances outside mate," I whispered to Nobby.

The geezer probably thought we were chancers who had descended on the area to take advantage of the riot. Many people from outside Handsworth had converged to either join in with the riots, or join in with the looting of the shops, which was taking police wherever the coppers had lost control. We made our way to the exit of the pub and opened the door which put us directly back into the action. The air was thick with smoke, blue lights were flashing through the haze, the sound of crashing bottles and the flash of exploding petrol lit up the night sky. Eventually the unrest made its way down the Villa Road, and we dodged our way back up the Soho Road and down Booth Street to the sanctuary of the Old Gate Inn. Steel Pulses' *Handsworth Revolution* was playing on the jukebox: "Had a good night lads?" asked Nobby's dad. "Yeah, if you like getting chased around the streets by the boys in blue," I answered sarcastically. "Are those idiots still rioting then?" He asked, "The police seem to be," replied Nobby. "No good for business having riots," replied Nobby's dad, "I've just thrown out two chancers who've never been in this bar since I've been here. Pair of mugs must be here for a free T.V or one of those new VCR machines I keep hearing about." I looked at Nobby and smiled. "Have you ever been in the Bee Hive dad?"

asked Nobby. "Funny you mention that because the gaffer of the joint called earlier saying a couple of mugs had been in causing trouble...must be the same pair who came in here." We looked at each other and laughed.

Nobby eventually gave me a ride home to Selly Oak on his Suzuki GT550 motorbike. The beast was like a little rocket because we covered the three or four miles in minutes, or so it seemed. We pulled up outside my mom's house, Nobby switched off the motor and took his helmet off. "This city is becoming a fucking joke mate," he said with a look of disappointment upon his face.
"Why? What do you mean? Because of what happened tonight, or just in general?" I replied.
"Well there are millions unemployed, all the big firms of closing down and it's all kicking off. So I suppose everything is shit at the moment," he said.
"Yeah, well there is fuck all we can really do about that mate. We've already tried in a couple of business ventures and the less said about that the better," I replied smiling. Nobby briefly smiled too. "Fucking hell, don't remind me of that! I'm just pissed off things are so hard. When are we gonna get a break?"
"Oh stop fucking moaning son. Surely our luck will change sooner rather than later. Anyway, what are your plans next week? If it is still bollocks over in Handsworth, come over here and we'll fuck off on the bikes somewhere." Nobby just looked at me, put on his skid lid, kick started the bike and fucked off down the road in a

cloud of smoke. "I have told him to lay off the fucking oil mix," I muttered smiling.

We had left school just a few years earlier and both of us were struggling like everybody else to find a decent job in a society, which had become fractured of late. Britain had recently gone through a difficult time, the Labour government had brought the country to her knees and now the Tory Party under the formidable Mrs Thatcher were trying to pick up the pieces. The riots weren't just confined to Handsworth either, it had been literally kicking off in: London, Liverpool and Manchester too. Many blamed Thatcher, however, it wasn't her fault at all. The 'Iron Lady'- as the Russians affectionately named her, took on the unions whom had caused so much disruption during the previous decade. Labour had quite literally bought British industry to its knees and Thatcher was determined to kick seven sorts of shit of them. She eventually did just that to the Marxist infested unions. They needed smashing at all costs; the financial burden of lost production caused by the never-ending strikes had to be addressed. Staunch far left unionists like 'Red Robbo' down at British Leyland in Birmingham are partially responsible for the collapse of the British motoring industry. Union disruption, lack of investment, and poor management ultimately brought the curtain down on many of the city's other industries. Birmingham, which proudly held the title of being the father of the industrial revolution and workshop of the world, now lay in tatters.

I bumped into Nobby a few weeks later on Corporation Street in Birmingham city centre. "Alright mate. Where the fuck are you going dressed like that? Are you getting married or something?" I asked. Nobby had a suit on you see, and the last time I had seen in such attire was back at school. Anyway, Nobby informed me he was going for a job interview and he asked me to come with him because he'd need a drink afterwards to calm his nerves. "Yeah OK why not. Where is your interview mate and what job have you applied for?" I asked inquisitively. "You ain't going to believe this mate, I've applied for a job in a fucking casino!" For a few seconds I had a look of surprise written across my face and then replied, "A casino? What the fuck are you going to do in a casino? Don't want to sound like a snob or anything Nobby, but you haven't exactly got the looks of James Bond." "Nay, not in the casino itself but parking the punters cars. Hopefully I'll be able to have a bash in some quality motors." I started laughing, "So you've applied for the job so you can fuck off in a flash motor?" He pulled a face and replied, "No, no, no....I'm not going to fucking nick one! But I reckon I will look the dogs bollocks driving around the city centre in a Ferrari or Porsche!" I was unsure. Who in their right mind would let Nobby loose in a hundred grand motor?

Anyway, several minutes later we were on Colmore Row in the financial district of the city looking for the joint, but we couldn't find it. However, standing outside

12

the Grand Hotel was a concierge looking rather dapper in his pink and grey uniform. "Excuse me my good man," said Nobby. The bloke casually looked in our direction and replied, "May one be of assistance, sir?"

"Yes, mush. Tell me…where is Cromwell's Casino?" The man took a few steps towards us and replied, "My name isn't '*mush*', sir, and you are standing next door to the casino!" We both span around and to our surprise, the posh speaking bellboy wasn't talking a load of old bollocks. The windows were all blacked out with a small sign saying 'Cromwell's Casino' in barely readable text written above the door. "I wonder why it's so inconspicuous?" I said to Nobby. "Fuck knows...well I suppose it's a private club and they don't want to attract any riff-raff," he replied. I smiled and immediately begun to have second thoughts about going into the joint. "Nobby, I will wait for you out here mate. I am not going down there dressed like this," I said. I looked at my appearance in the black mirrors and arrived at the conclusion I truly looked like a scruffy git in a pair of golden cords and leather jacket. Besides that, everybody walking along the street had suits on, so I already stood out like a sore thumb. "Oh stop being a poof! Just come down and wait for me; anyway, you ain't here to get a job so what does it matter?" he replied. I could see his point; after all, it was not me applying for a job. I did not possess a license anyway so I figured it made no difference what I actually looked like. "Yeah, you're right. Come on then, and good luck."

We were approaching the reception and some old geezer in a spotless tuxedo tried to block our path. The old fool certainly didn't appear amused to see us bounding down his stairs and you could almost read the dissatisfaction on his face. "Excuse me gentlemen, this happens to be a private members establishment. I have no recollection of either of you being patrons of this club?" Nobby put on his poshest of posh voices and replied, "My good fellow, I am here for a position within this fine establishment. Now, if you'd kindly step out of my way I have an appointment with the general manger." The grumpy old git looked Nobby up and down and smirked. Without moving an inch he replied, "And may I enquire as to what position is, 'sir' applying for?"
"I am here for the position of car jockey my good man, now kindly let me pass," retorted Nobby.
He grunted, peered over Nobby's shoulder and gave me the one over, "What, him too?" he quipped in a sarcastic tone. Cheeky old fucker, I thought but kept my gob shut. "My good man, this is a friend of mine. He is not here for a position within this fine establishment, he is simply going to wait until my business is concluded. Now kindly let us pass," replied Nobby, who was still trying to brow beat his foe with his confident attitude. I did not say a word; I just stood behind Nobby peering down on granddad who by now had suddenly softened his attitude.

The old fellow shook his head, stepped aside and told us both to, "sit down." He then effortlessly glided across the lobby picked up a phone, and then mumbled something incoherent on the other end.

Eventually a smiling face appeared from the doorway, a pleasant older woman who immediately melted the frosty atmosphere. She introduced herself as the casino general manager, and told Nobby to follow her. Just as they were about to disappear inside the building, she unexpectedly stopped. She span around with an inquisitive look and asked me with her eloquent voice, "Are you interested in a position as a trainee croupier too?" I was caught offside because the last thing I was expecting was a job interview. "No, no thank you," I replied timidly because I felt rather embarrassed by my scruffy appearance. More to the point, why was she asking about a trainee croupier's position? I thought Nobby was here to ponce about in some flash motors? Nobby looked at me in a surprised manner, his eyes widened, he shrugged his shoulders and lifted his hands, as if to say, "Fuck knows mate." Then she said, "Oh, I take it you are already working then, but give it a thought." Then they both disappeared behind one of the beautiful smoke glassed doors and into the main casino.

I looked up and the old guy was now standing behind his desk, staring down at me like an old school teacher whilst twiddling his moustache. You know when you're sitting a room and you think to yourself, "What the fuck am I doing here?" I did not want to make any eye contact with him, or get into any form of conversation with the old fossil; I just wanted Nobby to hurry the fuck up so we could go down pub. After a few agonizing minutes, he unexpectedly asked in a harsh voice, "And what exactly is it you do for a living sonny." Bollocks...he wants to start a conversation. "Oh nothing at the moment, I have just been laid off from a garage," I replied. "A garage? What were you a mechanic or something?" He asked with a raised voice. "Yes, but it didn't really suit me." I did not want to tell him the reason why I ended leaving, but it was definitely down the fact I was a useless mechanic. Neither did I want mention I had put a massive dent in the bosses Porsche by dropping the lid of a wheel-balancing machine on to it, which did not go down too well. Fortunately, the car jockey returned from parking one of the punters cars, and his warm smile quickly melted away the awkward atmosphere. He was telling the old man about the goings on behind the hotel, "Just pranged old Beastons' Jag," he said. "How on earth did you manage that?" asked the old man. "Well as I was reversing into the lot, some bloke had his skirt up adjusting his suspender belt," he replied laughing. "Some bloke? Surely you mean a woman?" "Nah, I have never seen a bird around here wearing white Y-Fronts and wearing a pair of stilettos bigger than my size elevens," he replied whilst pointing to his foot that he had firmly placed on the reception desk. The old man shook his head and for a brief moment, a smiled emerged across his face. "After 30yrs working around here, nothing surprises me anymore," he said. The car jockey then turned around and asked me, "Are you here for the job too son?"

"Nah mate, I have no driving licence."

"Driving licence? The jobs on offer are for casino dealers mate," he replied. "I know nothing about casinos, I am only here because I bumped into my mate by pure chance, and I am just waiting for him. And I am sure he said the position was for a car jockey," I replied. "But since you're here, you might as well have a bash. Anyway, it's a good laugh here. I am sure you'll like it son," he replied. "What *is* a dealers post?" I asked. The car jockey laughed and replied, "Dealing man! Dealing roulette and blackjack to the punters!" Dealing? What the fuck did I know about dealing? However, several minutes of gentle persuasion, they somehow managed to talk me into applying. "You'll be OK. They are looking for quiet people like you," said the car jockey. A grin developed across my face. 'If only these fuckers knew,' I thought. "Tell me one thing though; why don't they just place an advert in the newspapers for casino dealers? My mate was under the impression he'd come here for the car jockey job," I asked. The two men looked at each other and a few seconds later let out roars of laughter. 'Fuck me am I in some sort of madhouse?' After they had both stopped laughing, the receptionist picked up the phone, and again mumbled something inaudible under his breath. He then put the phone down, raised his head and gave me a cheeky smile. I just sat there like a plum and shrugged my shoulders.

Two minutes later, the door of the casino swung open and the casino GM and Nobby reappeared both smiling and shaking hands. "Thank you for attending. You're exactly the sort of person we're looking for. Now if you would kindly take a seat, I shall interview your friend." Nobby immediately looked at me and a huge grin developed across his face. "Please get one of the girls to bring Paul some sandwiches and a drink," she said to the receptionist. She then turned to me, smiled and said, "Well, it appears my staff are more convincing in attracting potential employees than I am." I arose from my seat, smiled and shook her hand, "Hello, you caught me off guard earlier because the last thing I was expecting today was an interview, hence the way I look, nice to meet you, my name is Windmill," I said. "Hello Windmill, I'm sure you'll brush up like an old penny. Now if you'd kindly follow me please we will get down to business." She glided across the floor and opened the door to a business I would eventually be involved in for a quarter of a century.

Twenty minutes later, we were all shaking hands on the reception. Both of us had been offered positions as trainee croupiers. Outside the joint, we looked at each other stunned for a few minutes. "How the fuck did that just happen?" I asked. "Fuck knows mate, it must be our lucky day. Come on, let's go and have a pint to celebrate, and it is your round," he said with a beaming smile. Once in the pub, and the round bought, I asked him, "What on earth possessed you to apply for a position within a casino in the first place anyway?"

"Well, to be honest as you already know, I had not applied for a position has a trainee dealer. I went there to get a job as the car jockey mate. The GM said they were doing a training school and thought I'd be much more suitable for that position." I sat there and thought about what he had just said. "Those two on reception mentioned they put the car jockey position up to attract applications, I wonder why?" I replied. "Fuck knows," said Nobby. Anyway, that did not really matter to either of us right now. Two weeks later we turned up for our first training session within the joint. The interior of the casino certainly resembled everything you have probably seen on TV. Namely, dim lights, sparkling roulette wheels, opulent decorations, and extraordinarily good painting on the walls. It all looked incredibly impressive for us novices.

Only four people turned up for the preliminary training class. Nobby, me, a fella called Vince, and another bloke who happened to be cross-eyed. The training classes were scheduled to last for six weeks and they started from 10am in the morning until 6pm five days a week. The actual casino itself did not open to the public until two in the afternoon; therefore, the casino was deserted in the mornings. The training officer was a fat bastard called

Terry, he looked a bit sleazy to be frank with a big
moustache and short black curly hair. He also had a look
in his eyes that said, 'fuck you lot. I do not actually give a
shit about all this,' and as things turned out, he really did
not give two fucks about anything. Therefore, the initial
perception did not offer any signs of encouragement for
either of us from day one; however, we were new in the
joint so we could put up with his arrogance for the time
being. He was the exact opposite of the friendly GM who
gave us the jobs. Perhaps she was the sweetener to get
people through the door and now the slave master was
going to whip us into shape. I think Nobby was privately
relieved that he had bumped into me a few weeks
previously because the thought of being stuck in a room
with this bunch would have made him take an early bath,
and hit the exit door giving all the customary salute with
his middle finger. Upstairs on a break from the training he
said, "What do you think?" "Well, not too sure about the
attitude of Terry to be honest. He seems to be a right
arrogant twat."
"Yeah I have to agree, if he starts getting lippy we'll jump
over the table and do the fucker," he replied laughing. The
caretaker guy was upstairs too having a coffee break, and
he asked what we though of the job so far. He told us to
take no notice of Terry either because he had probably
been in the running the pit last night. "What the fucking
hell is the pit?" I asked. The geezer laughed and replied,
"You fucking lumpies! The pit is a name for a group of

tables. Here we have four pits. Oh, and a lumpy is the name given to trainee dealers like you lot!"

"Ooh OK...and you mean he didn't get off until about 4am this morning and is now back here at 10am?" replied Nobby. No wonder he was such a miserable fucker.

Later that afternoon Terry informed the four trainees standing around the roulette table, "Once the trainings finished, you fuckers will have to take different jobs in the casino until your gaming licences arrive. One of you will be on reception, one of you will be on the valet, one parking the punters cars and, the other behind the bar. Now, which one is which?" We immediately grinned at each other and shouted in unison, "I'll take the bar!" However, I soon changed my option after seeing one of the valet girls come out of the kitchens in her skin-tight dress. I immediately opted for the valet instead. "I would prefer the valet actually Terry. My mother once ran a sandwich shop," I said. Nobby looked perplexed and whispered, "What do you mean? Where exactly was this shop you bullshitter?" he said. "Sush, you know my mom used to make all the sandwiches when we fucked off down to Cornwall. I used to help her," I replied smiling. "Fuck off! You never made any of those sarnies you bullshitting bastard," he retorted. "Oh shut up! You'll be better off behind the bar anyway," I replied. "Why?" He asked. "Because I have already told Terry your old man runs several pub. Anyway, the valet girls have to go to the bar to fetch the players drinks. Think about it for a second

Nobby; the bar is always dead, so you'll have plenty of chances to chat them all up! Plus you can watch TV all night whilst I will be slogging away on the gaming floor," I replied. Nobby thought about the situation for several seconds and agreed. This was a good thing too, because I eventually ended up having a real good time with the girls in the kitchen. Several weeks later, Nobby was stuck behind the bar bored shitless because the TV was broken, even worse, the valet girls hardly went up there because most of the punters in the joint didn't drink. The guy with the cross-eyes was given the post as the car jockey and Vince was lumbered with the old git on reception.

One day the usual car jockey had not shown up for his shift, rumour had it he pulled the she male behind the hotel the previous night and was upstairs in one of the hotel rooms having the living fudge packed out of him. Well that was the gossip in the staffroom because somebody coming in for their shift seen him leaving the hotel holding his arse. Therefore, the trainee allocated that particular post was excused from class so he could park the punters cars. This was the last time we would see our cross-eyed friend in the casino. He had a serious accident parking one of the cars and was subsequently rushed to intensive care. Now because of his unfortunate accident with a lamppost this only left Nobby, Vince and me. Vince turned out to be a champion, a champion fucking bullshitter! Nobby and I just could not believe all the drivel that spewed from his gob. Even so, he made it worthwhile turning up for the training because you just had no idea of the crap that he would come out with that particular day.

One day Vince said, "The only reason I'm doing the training school is because my girlfriend has a job on a cruise ship. She is a hairdresser and I'm leaving immediately after the training to join her." Me and Nobby looked at each other puzzled. "Sorry to sound stupid Vince, but what as that got to do with you being in a casino?" asked Nobby. "The missus told me that all I need to do is learn the basics because the casinos are very quiet and the casino is the easiest place to get a job," replied Vince enthusiastically. Nobby and I looked at each other with scepticism. We had perfected the look down to a tee, and whenever we felt somebody was talking a load of bollocks, we would give each other a look to confirm our agreement. Vince also informed us that he only needed to complete the blackjack class, because apparently the Americans did not play roulette. We thought this rather odd to say the least, but we could not argue with him because we did not know either, however, if what he was saying were actually true, why would the ships bother installing roulette tables in the first place?

The training was going okay; it was not exactly rocket science adding up a random combination of bets, however, poor old Vince had become a lost cause. He insisted whilst Terry was not around, "Do not place any big bets on the layout because it is a pointless exercise as far as I am concerned." Me and Nobby just looked at each other, said "OK Vince," and then we proceeded to put even larger bets all over the layout. "What did I just fucking tell you two?" shouted Vince who was suddenly becoming very angry. I will never forget the look on his face whilst he was screaming at the top of his voice: "*No more fuckin bets you bastards!*" This obviously caught the attention of Terry who was trying to get some kip down the other end of pit. "Oi, what the hell is going on over there?" he shouted. "Oh shit, that's blown it," whispered Vince. On his way over to the roulette table to see what was happening the ball dropped into number 23, which was covered in huge bets. "Bollocks," shouted Vince. Terry looked puzzled and asked him, "What's the problem Vince? On a live game it is a lot more hectic than this." Vince had a myriad of excuses at the ready and replied, "I'm not interested because I plan to get a job on a cruise ship once I have learnt blackjack because the Americans do not play roulette." Terry looked surprised and replied, "Really Vince, and who as told you all of this?" "My missus. She works on a ship in the Caribbean in the beauty salon, and she said she'd never seen anybody playing roulette whilst passing through the casino on her way to the crew bar," replied Vince.

Terry started pulling some extraordinary faces; he did not say anything. He just turned around and burst out in hysterical laughter. Nobby and I did not join in just in case he jumped over the table and chinned us for taking the piss. Vince's loopy logic came to harvest in the final week of tuition, he suffered the humiliation of the sack for refusing to add up any roulette bets. Therefore, even the though the original training school only had four people, only me and Nobby had survived the course. Once we'd finished and were awaiting our gaming licenses to arrive, we took up our designated posts within the casino.

Nobby headed towards the bar and I headed towards the kitchen to join all the sexy valet girls. I spent a few months in the kitchen and the girls turned out to be great fun. The head chef was a complete nutter, perpetually throwing crockery and burnt offerings of food around the kitchen whilst screaming like a lunatic. Janice, Robyn, and Lucy were radiant girls who were always up to mischief, they were a real hoot. Robyn had a sister there too, but I cannot remember her name now. Imagine being wedged in a smallish kitchen with these beautiful women of all different colours in skimpy little dresses, which incidentally clung to every curve of their voluptuous bodies. Boy, oh boy were they funny; Janice was the wildest of the bunch and she just oozed sexuality. These girls knew their stuff and Janice could do things with a cucumber I had never thought possible!

Since it was now approaching Christmas, the general manager informed the whole casino we could wear fancy dress for a night if we desired. The girls in the kitchen immediately suggested I don one of their dresses. "Good idea," I said. Little did they know I had been planning to get into all of their dresses at some point. Robyn said, "Come around to my apartment tomorrow an hour before work and I will sort you out." The next night I somehow managed to squeeze into her spare dress; she had also purchased a long black curly wig for me to wear and it fitted like a fucking glove. Whilst she was applying my make-up she was literally in fits of hysterical laughter. "What the fuck is so funny? Do you reckon the punters will clock it straight away?" I asked her. "Just don't sit down mate," she said laughing whist pointing to the lump between me legs. "You'll give the game away!"

That night at work was brilliant; Nobby turned up as a gorilla and all the girls from the valet turned up as the cast of St Trinians. They sure knew how to work the crowd with their seductive looks and because they were allowed to accept tips, they undoubtedly made a lot more than the dealers. Later that night in the kitchen Janice collared me, "So are you actually going to go on the tables when your licence arrives Windmill, or are you staying in here with me?" she asked. She then bent right over picking something up off a bottom shelf and since she had the shortest skirt and black stockings on, I got a real eyeful. She looked back giving me one of her cheeky grins. My god she had a fine ass and she would constantly swing it your way if she got the chance. I stepped forward and gave it a right good slap, "If you promise to stay in that position baby, I will stay in the kitchen indefinitely," I roared. Next thing I knew she was thrusting her ass into my crutch, rubbing it up and down against me, so I grabbed her hips and simulated the act. At that the moment the GM entered, "Janice, can I...oh dear, I will come back later," she giggled and walked back out. My face went as red as a tomato and Janice burst out laughing. She quickly got up, swung around and put her arms around me, "You see honey, Janice will take care of you." Bob the chef then came in carrying the vegetables he needed to cook for the evening meals. "Oi, you two, none of that in here please. This is a respectable establishment and I don't want you breaking all my plates on the table," he said smiling. Janice gave me a kiss on the cheek, smiled and said, "Go take a break honey, and we shall resume this later. I may even take you home tonight sweety so we can get things straight between us." To say I was slightly hot under the collar would be the under statement of the decade. I quickly left the kitchen and made my way towards the staff room to cool down a bit.

After Christmas our licenses arrived and it was time to go onto the live games. It was harrowing at first because I had been thinking more about the girls over the previous few months and I had virtually forgotten all that training malarkey. All the regular players were like sharks on a feeding frenzy once a new trainee hit the live games. They knew we were vulnerable to making mistakes.

27

Taking off winning bets, clearing wrong numbers and losing control of the games. It did not take long to suss out the punters either. Most were here to screw the casino for as much money as they could get their hands on, and that meant by any means necessary to stack the odds in their favour.

The first few weeks were a complete blur for both Nobby and me, we were still trying to find our feet and learn the ropes. The initial pre perceptions of the casino business however, appeared to be unfounded. The only beautiful women in the joint were the waitresses; there weren't any James Bond types coming through the doors with wads of cash, just loads of immigrants in for the free sandwiches and drinks. Seems crazy now thinking about these days. We worked 5 days a week from 8pm until 4am in the morning - including weekends, for £55 per week. Naturally Saturday and Sundays were the busiest nights, so your days off would usually be Monday and Tuesday, but at least you were more or less guaranteed a day shift – 12 noon till 8pm, before your days off. However, the pay was shite considering the unsociable hours, and many casino dealers of the era fucked off to other joints for a few pounds per week more, or even abroad.

Several months later back in the casino I was beginning to hate some of the managers in Cromwell's, especially a big double barrel named prick named, Isaac Hugh Hunt. What a pompous wanker, forever moaning if somebody actually had the cheek to win some money on his shift. I am not talking about huge sums either, even if one of the players requested a few £5 chips with the winning payout this manager would insist on passing out as much colour as possible. His reasoning being the player(s) would stash the cash chips and gamble back the table chips. So with the dealers taking all the abuse, "Oi you fucker...didn't I tell you to pass me some cash chips with that payout? Are you fucking deaf?" Dealers had to stand there and take all the abuse whilst he stood there laughing. You probably won't understand this but back then, the casino management let the players talk to the staff like shit because they were spending money in the casino, and when I say talk to the staff like shit, I mean just that. Nobby and me never knew any better because we'd never been in any casino prior to Cromwell's. The atmosphere in the casino was the complete opposite of what you would have expected. It really was a 'us' verses 'them' scenario. You simply ignored the punters and avoided any unnecessary communication with them. If a player started being friendly and wanting to talk, you could guarantee he was testing you out to place him some illegal bets, or sweetening you up to make you an offer of a scam.

One night this Arab mother-fucker bought in for £5000 and lost most of it within twenty minutes. With only a few £25 chips to play, he hit a number straight up which pays 35/1. Mr. Hunt was inspecting the game, and I asked for him to check the payout of £1750 was correct. The look on the fat fuckers face was worth its weight in gold; you could see the steam coming out of his ears. "Check" he shouted whilst biting his lip and muttered, "you cunt," under his pig breath. I looked at him, smiled and replied, "Sweating a bit aren't you? Is that lucky rabbits foot you keep in your pocket stuck up your arse or something?" Well from that day forward we never really saw eye to eye. I did not really like the fat fucker anyway, and I let Nobby know I would be on my way soon to check out the other joints. The reason for this is quite simple.

Once you work in casinos you become apart of a secret little society as such, and dealers from the other casinos used to congregate in a snooker club after work called Churchill's in town. You soon learnt that as you gained experience in the business, you could then literally walk out of one casino and into another for a few quid per shift more per week. "They're all the same mate," said one lad, "why work down at that shithole with those wankers when you can work at our shithole with our wankers for more pay?" He had a point. If you're resigned to putting up with all the bollocks you may as well get paid for all the grief. This geezer seemed OK, and he insisted I applied to the Midland Wheel Club on the Hagley Road. On my next days off I turned up at the joint and was offered a job immediately, for a few quid per shift more per week.

Before I left Cromwell's, another training school had just finished and a young man by the name of Bob

Jenkins made his way onto the casino floor. Nobby and I had no idea at the time, but he was hilarious. The geezer had only been in the casino for three weeks when he nearly burnt down the staffroom. After the fire brigade had doused the inferno, one of the fire fighters lined all the casino staff up and asked, "Whose is this jacket?" "That's mine," replied the Bob timidly. His zippo petrol lighter had somehow started the fire. They suspected he forgot to put the fucking out whilst rushing back to the casino floor after smoking a fag. "Some fucker must have used it, I don't even smoke," he said. Nobby and I gave each other one of 'those' looks. "You are not any relation to a bloke called Vince are you?" asked Nobby. "I do have a cousin called Vince," replied the Bob, "he's just got a job on a cruise ship shovelling shit down the galley."

The Midland Wheel Club was different class to Cromwell's; the managers were all cool and the staff even cooler. We had some suave staff here who were ice cool. The casino was actually very exclusive. It was 1986, and the gaffer of the joint was a Brummie chap and a self-made millionaire called Alan Manning. His brother, Patsy was once a gangster and boxer in the seedier side of life but a great bloke – as long as you never crossed him. His brother Alan was a very charming and influential in Birmingham; the bourgeois clientele affirmed his social standing with their attendance. The place was full of businessmen, lawyers and the such. Unlike Cromwell's, you could not get into the Wheel unless you had a suit on, even in the afternoon. The place was so relaxed and easy going it really was a pleasure to work here. The general manager – Gloria, was as cool as the other one over at Crowell's, but crucially, her mangers' weren't wankers.

I met some decent lads here, one named La Bamba. All was good for a few months, the casino was so relaxed and the atmosphere so cool it almost seemed too good to be true. As things turned out it was, because for some mysterious reason the boss of the casino decided to hire a twat called Albert Bundy. To this very day, I am not sure why the powers that be inside the Midland Wheel employed this man. His methods of management were abysmal in comparison to the others in the job. It seemed like his only method of management was to wind up the staff and create a them v me atmosphere, remarkably like Mr. Hunt back at Cromwell's. Experience tells you it only takes one bellend to upset any given group of people. For example, you might be on the piss with your mates and some cock comes along and ruins the whole night, or you may be sunbathing and a suddenly a dark cloud appears out of nowhere to cover the sunlight – or some other shit, but you get the drift. I am not a violent person, neither do I condone any form of physical violence, however, I was hoping someone would knock him the fuck out.

Anyway, to cut a long story short this Bundy fellow pissed off a considerable amount of the staff, and a few of us fucked off 300 yards down the road to secure employment at the legendary Rainbow Casino. Not long after our arrival at the Rainbow, we heard through the grapevine the owner of the Wheel had fired Bundy because he had managed to fracture the whole casino with his loopy management methods. This is how simple it is to lose your best staff, in fact all your staff. Just employ a dickhead and the job is a good one. Retribution would be awaiting Bundy several years later for his arrogance on the high seas; however, that can wait for now. Getting back to the Rainbow, it really was the place to be at this particular time. The joint was always packed with punters, and full of nutters. The first joint had more than a few bellends in management places; the Wheel was definitely better and a lot more sophisticated than Crowell's, however, Bundy soon fucked all that up, so now here I was at the Rainbow to try my luck. I had only been here for a few months when I received promotion to Inspector. Basically, this means when a dealer reaches a competent level, he/she moves up the ladder in the casino world and watches the action on the games, rather than constantly deal them all night. What usually happens in the casinos is experienced dealers end up going on all the busiest games the trainee dealers cannot handle. After a while, you get sick and tired of dealing all night, and once a casino as a satisfactory amount of competent dealers, the reward them with pay rises and positions where they do not have to deal heaving games all the time. In effect to make life slightly easier. Working in casinos isn't physical work though you understand, its just the ability to add up different combinations of wagers and talk a load of shite.

They had a dice game at the Rainbow and a sound geezer called Stuart Reading was the boxman. They also had a funny looking mother fucker running the pit called Nick, a tall skinny geezer whom everybody thought was in the closet, as things turned out they were all right. The year was 1987, and working in the Rainbow could be chaotic. Talking about dealing heaving games, I remember dealing roulette one night with loads of Chinese people, when unexpectedly one of the older ones had a stroke or heart attack at the table. Not one of his companions checked to see if he was okay, they just all stopped playing for a split second, looked at him on the floor, and then started making bets amongst themselves that he would not make it to the hospital! I am not joking either. Chinese people are crazy about gambling and they are not afraid to make huge wagers when their numbers start hitting home. Out of all the casinos in Birmingham, this joint was renowned throughout the entire UK gaming industry. The assortment of characters who have passed through the doors working the tables is extraordinary, the club has produced so many staff who have gone on around the world to run casinos is testimony to its legendary status with the casino industry. Stuart Reading was perhaps one of the finest, and I would end up working with him during my career in many parts of the world.

The general manager of the joint - a bloke named Reg, was a cool dude too. He had a soft spot for me because in my youth I used to race motocross: AMCA (*Amateur Motor Cycle Association*) Mugen Honda CR125 for the Moseley Club in Birmingham. Reg loved motorcycles too, and he knew the legendary Vale Onslow of Birmingham. The man was famous in the UK for his exploits on bikes and his shop on the Strafford Road was a Mecca for all the hairy bastards with leather jackets. I actually sold him a Triumph Tiger Cub 200cc a few years earlier, which to this day was perhaps the biggest mistake I had ever made. The bike without question was the best machine I had ever owned and today that same bike is worth a lot of money. Unfortunately, what Reg did not realize was the fact that I preferred to party more than I liked work during this time in my life. I was still a kid really and this meant I'd prefer being with my mates down the pub. One night, I arrived at the joint without having a shave after spending all day in bed recovering from the previous nights exploits. Nick the pit boss was not too happy and he said, "Oi, you cannot come into the pit on my shift looking like a bag of grit! Go upstairs now and have a shave." I told him that I had no razor with me and he said he would find me one. Anyway, eventually he turned up with a blade and I went upstairs to do the job in hand, but I only had time to shave exactly half of my face. The phone in staff room rang, and Nick said, "Get down to the pit now! We need you to watch a couple of games."

"But Nick..." I was interrupted, "No fucking ifs or fucking buts! Get your arse down here now or you'll be even more fucking trouble." He then hung up the phone. When I arrived back in the pit Nick was not there, but the other pit boss Jimbo said, "Hitler wants you watch roulette's one and two." I shrugged my shoulders and started to make my way down the pit. "Hold on a minute," he said and began to peer at my face. "You fucking nutter," he said laughing, "you know he'll go ape-shit when he sees that!" "So fucking what," I replied. "I was trying to him, but he hung up." Anyway I had to pass all the other dealers and inspectors and they all clocked it straight away and started laughing. "You know he's going to kick off when he sees that," said the inspector I had to relieve. "Listen pal," I said, "I know what a company boy Hitler is, and there is only one fucking option available." The inspector started laughing and replied, "you crafty fucker! It's only 8-30. You've done that so you can get suspended for the evening!" I winked at him and awaited the inevitable uproar when Adolf returned.

The punters in this joint were just as miserable as the fuckers down at Cromwell's. I am sure most of them just wanted to escape from their wives back home for a few hours. A few of the hardcore regulars would sit around one of the empty blackjack tables and moan about anything and everything. Nick suddenly appeared over by the men's bogs. He came prancing over to the pit, jumped over the ropes, gave me a quick glance and said, "Good boy." Two minutes later and he was back again. "How much is Mr. Easton in for?" Meaning how much money had a player named Easton spent so far. I looked at the sheet and replied, "According to this £550. he hasn't bought in for any more cash since I arrived." Unfortunately, Hitler was standing on the 'shaven' side of my face and never noticed the other half. "Bollocks," I said. Hitler looked at me and asked, "what's the fucking matter now?" I turned around and pointed to a table over on the other side of the casino, "I knocked a coffee over on that table over there in my rush to get down here. You wouldn't fuck off over and clean it up for me would you?" I bit my lip and awaited the response. Suddenly his eyes squinted and his head moved closer to mine, I have never seen anybody's face explode into a mixture of colours quite like that before. "Are you taking the fucking piss!" he screamed. "Sorry mate, I was half way through when you called. I tried to explain, but you put the phone down," I replied. "Don't give me that bullshit! You were up there for twenty minutes! Go on, in the fucking office! You're having a disciplinary!" Jimbo turned up a few minutes later and he could hardly keep a straight face. He said, "Windmill you sneaky bastard you're suspended for one day starting from tonight because of your blatant disregard for military orders!" I grinned because I already knew I'd get the night off. I'd learnt all the tricks of the trade off my work mates who had a variety of scams to get suspended for the evening. Plenty of them just seemed to turn up when they wanted and now because I figured the GM was on my side, I too would see how far I could push the boat out. One fucker even turned up for his shift, went into the staff room opened the window, climbed out and shimmy'd down the drainpipe. "Oi,"shouted one of where the fucking hell are you going?" Asked a dealer. "To the fucking pub," the reply. I eventually ended up having a folder full of written and final written warnings from the Rainbow. I think I held the all time record for actually receiving four final written warnings for my time and attendance. When I finally returned to work Reg summoned me to his office and screamed, "I am telling you now. If you miss one more fucking shift you're out!" I had never seen him so angry before, I guess he felt I was taking the piss out of him personally because we had become mates.

Nobby called later that week, he was still at Cromwell's Casino, "Oi Windmill, do you fancy going for a job interview?" he asked. "Yeah I'm on my last legs here mate. Where?"

"Africa," he replied.

"Africa? I saw that advertised in the paper the other day. Where are the interviews?"

"Manchester, I am going to call them," Replied Nobby.

"OK, let me know the score. Tell them I am coming up too. Oh, you better put Bob's name on the list as well," I said. Two weeks later, were in Manchester for an interview with a company named Sun International. The actual casino we were applying for was called Sun City and the hotel/casino was located in a place called Bophuthatswana in South Africa. The geezer doing the interviews was the GM from Sun City; I will never forget meeting him because he was such a character. It is a shame we never actually worked under him because he left the company shortly before the three amigos arrived there. During the interview, this is exactly what he said:"What's your name son?"

"Windmill," I answered.

"Right you fucker, do you deal roulette and blackjack?"

"Yes I do,"

"Do you like women and drinking?"

"Fucking right I do," I retorted.

"Right you've got the job; I'll send you a letter in the post, now send the next fucker in." He replied.

This was the first and only conversation I ever had with the man. Even so, I soon learnt once in Africa he was a legend, I could see why. I went in to see Reg at the Rainbow and handed in my notice. I apologized for my disruptive behaviour over the last few months and made the peace. Reg was cool though and he said, "Good luck son, and you know you can come back to this joint whenever you like. Just try and behave yourself over there, they will not be as tolerant to your timekeeping as we have been here." We shook hands, and I said my farewells to all the staff at the Rainbow. I had learnt a lot about the business here, and without doubt, I would use that knowledge to my advantage in Africa. Therefore, that was that. The three of us were all booked on the same direct flight from Heathrow in May 1987 to Johannesburg in South Africa.

THE ROAD TO SUN CITY

I was sitting on the plane trying to figure out what was going on because just two years previous, I never even had a job. Now here I was with three mates sitting on a jumbo jet heading to Namibia and South Africa all expenses paid. It was my first time flying and I felt excited - well for a short while anyway, because the excitement soon turned to boredom after the initial take off. I quickly realised I would be stuck within a tin can flying through the air at 500mph for the next twelve hours of my life, what a bitch eh?

Once the plane took off – and whilst Bob was christening the planes shithouse, Nobby was telling me Bob could spin a yarn or two just like Vince whilst they were both at Cromwell's, so now the three of us had a considerable amount of time in each others company, it was time to see if Nobby was telling the truth. Nobby reckoned Bob could bullshit for England if they ever have such a discipline in the Olympics. He said he was that good at it, he even believed all the waffle himself.
A few minutes after Bob returned from the crapper he suddenly started telling us that he had learnt to fly at the age of twelve, taught by no other than Barnes Wallis on 1

November 1979.

"Really Bob," said Nobby, "funny how you haven't mentioned any of this before," with a hint of sarcasm in his voice. He then whispered to me, "You know who Barnes Wallis is right?"

Of course I bloody well knew! He was the fella who invented an underwater rocket, every idiot knew that.

"Bob, excuse my ignorance, but didn't Wallis invent The Rocket?" I asked.

"No, no that was Isambard Kingdom Brunel on the Liverpool to Manchester," replied Bob.

By now Nobby had a bemused look on his face and said,"What the hell are you two going on about?"

"My dad used to take me to school on The Rocket," replied Bob.

"Your dad used to take you to school on The Rocket? Absolute bollocks Bob! Rocket ain't run for over a hundred years and anyway, you went to school in Birmingham, not Liverpool or Manchester! So how do work that one out then?" Nobby retorted.

"Oh yes he did! It had three cylinders and he brought it brand new in 1968," replied Bob.

Nobby and I looked at each other in confusion.

"Bob, what the hell are you going on about now? What sort of rocket are you on about?" asked Nobby.

"A *BSA* Rocket," replied Bob.

"Let me get this straight. You're telling us your old man used to take you to school on a 1968 BSA Rocket motorcycle?" I asked.

"And what the fucking hell has that got to do with Barnes
Wallis or Isambard kingdom Brunel?" added Nobby.

"I never said The Rocket had anything to do with Wallis.
Windmill said that, I thought he was talking about the
famous train that Brunel and Trevithick designed for the
Liverpool to Manchester Railway," replied Bob.

We were convinced Bob was talking a load of bollocks,
however, we were oblivious to the historical engineering
achievements of by-gone days so could not really refute
his arguments. "Excuse me gents," said Bob, "Not sure if
I should have had last nights curry for breakfast...I'm
touching fucking cloth here!" He suddenly jumped up and
ran down the isle to use the crapper. Whilst he was away
some bloke sitting opposite said, "Your mate is talking a
complete load of shite." We were about to find out more
when the Bob suddenly returned from the thunder-box.
"Tell me Bob, what do you think of the politics of South
Africa?" asked Nobby. Bob had the opinion Charles
Darwin had no idea what he was talking about and his
theories' were all wrong. Man, according to Bob, evolved
from spiders. "What the fuck are you going on about
now?" I replied. Many conversations of this nature took
place as we slowly made our way down the coast of
Africa and towards Namibia. On several occasions, the
sexy flight attendants' politely told us to keep our heated
debates down. At point, Bob had the whole back of
the plane arguing over his insistence that South Africa,

along with America, were still British. In fact, one bloke who was from South Africa wanted to punch his fucking lights out. However, I immediately recognized the comical situation and said to Bob, "Go on Bob, offer him to step outside for a fucking fight!"

Several hours later we landed in South West Africa – Namibia, at a place called Windhoek to pick up fuel. Shortly afterwards, the iron lump was back up in the blue skies for the final leg of our journey. Less than two hours later we were flying over the City of Johannesburg, the three of us were now having a scrap for the window to see what was outside. Johannesburg is a big city, much bigger than Birmingham. The plane done its tips and turns and then suddenly we were on the ground; heading for customs. Customs were taking forever, the fella sitting behind the protective glass was going through my passport with intense scrutiny. I found peculiar because this was my first trip abroad and there was absolutely nothing in the passport. Finally his stony face looked up and without a smile or a thank you, he handed me back my documentation. Bob and Nobby suffered the same shit. Once outside the terminal, a black fella picked us up in his combi - an African taxi, and we now had a three-hour drive to Sun City. Prior to my arrival here, I had done some research on South Africa to see what was actually going on in the country. South Africa at this time was still under apartheid, which meant blacks and whites were separated. Since we all came from the cultural melting pot of Birmingham, it seemed bizarre. So to be actually in South Africa and see it with your own eyes was surreal in many ways.

After we had left Jo'burg, we were in a new world that humbled us because the drive across South Africa towards Sun City was brilliant. The sheer size of the country is astounding compared to tiny little England. Huge, and I mean huge expanses of wilderness with nothing but never ending plains and extinct volcanoes. We could have been transported back in time for all I knew, it was extraordinary. All of us were still bewildered by what was going on outside the window of the Combi, when all of a sudden a great big cowboy appeared out of nowhere on the side of the road. I do not mean a real cowboy, this was a fifty-foot neon sort of sign. Just like the famous one you've probably seen on the TV programmes from Las Vegas. Sun City is located on the outer ring of the Pilannesburg ring of mountains and these mountains are actually an extinct crop of volcanoes. How Sol Kezner had the vision to dream up and build this resort in the middle of nowhere is astonishing to say the least. Suddenly all the dry bush and half-looking dead trees outside the entrance of the complex had been replaced with lush, almost tropical looking trees and vegetation of every description. Towering hotels could be seen behind the lush palm trees. "Fucking hell Nobby," I said, "how much did it cost to build all this?" Nobby looked around in awe, "I have no idea, but at a guess I'd say hundreds of millions." The driver of the combi looked in his rear-view mirror and said, "Sol built everything. There wasn't even any roads into this place until he came."

One of the representatives of the company met us as we pulled up outside one of the hotels. She introduced herself and said, "Welcome to Sun City! You will be staying in the Cabanas Hotel until your staff quarters' are ready. We apologize about this but they need some essential maintenance." Me and Nobby looked at each other and grinned. "Oh how awful," replied Nobby with his usual sarcasm. Anyway, during the evening we all had a good look around the complex and were staggered by the sheer size of the resort. There was nothing back in the UK that even came close to this place, or any place that you could compare it to either. Thousands of people worked in Sun City, the complex was crowded with people from all over the globe and everybody looked like they were having the time of their lives.

"Fuck me Nobby, this place is going to take some getting used to," I said.

"Mate, how fucking cool is it to be here? I mean, just imagine being stuck in Cromwell's right now with all those miserable wankers moaning?"

Nobby was right, there was something in the air here. You could taste the excitement and we were about to get involved in all the action.

After a few days we got assigned to our staff apartment, it was on the second level and right at the end of the compound. It was cool, it had all the stuff you would find in an apartment: a fridge for the beer, a bed for shagging and a crapper for doing what boys do best.

I will never forget the first day in the place because Nobby opened the windows and immediately looked shocked. I asked him what the problem was and he just stood there waving his arms, signalling me to come over to the window. "Wow," I roared, I could not believe what I was seeing. Sitting on the fence directly below our place were three vervat monkeys, just sitting there looking up towards us, one of them even looked like Bob.

"You've read the Metamorphoses by Ovid haven't you Nobby?" I asked. "Yes mate I have, why?" Replied Nobby. "Well it hasn't taken too long for the Bob to make the transformation," whilst pointing to the biggest monkey on the fence. Nobby suddenly disappeared and returned a few seconds later with his arms full. We had been shopping earlier in the staff shop and had brought loads of fruits, so naturally we started to feed our newfound African friends with the bananas. This soon turned into a calamity because within minutes there were loads of the furry little fuckers everywhere. We did not know it at the time, but it was strictly against company policy to feed any of the wildlife because they were such a nuisance to the whole complex. We later discovered that once the vervat monkeys turn up and start making a racket; this attracts the larger baboons and they are apparently quite dangerous. Later we heard a story of one of the girls on the lower levels going to sleep after a night on the lash in the staff pub, only to forget to close her sliding double doors that lead out to the staff swimming pool. She got a rude awakening to find a great big stinking baboon in her apartment instead of her boyfriend. I can picture it now, her asleep and the baboon jumping into the scratcher next to her, "Hello love, where have you been all night..."

Anyway, we got a ticking off from other members of staff, but they let it pass because they knew we were fresh boys out of the city and still wet behind the ears.

The first night of work was crazy and the casino was huge. God knows how many staff worked in there, but at a quick guess hundreds. Back in England the casinos carry on average around thirty staff, here you had more than that amount on a break at any given time and, the staff room alone was the size of the average casino in England. There were loads of good-looking women too; typical eighties look: birds nest hairstyles and plastered in make-up. "Mate, we are onto a winner here," I said to Nobby whilst we made our way through the casino, "what do you mean?" he replied. "Have a look around you you daft git!" Nobby looked puzzled. "Oh for fucks sake dumbo! The women!" I said. I was beginning to wonder if Nobby liked packing fudge because he never seemed interested in the fruits of the casinos. It was the same at Cromwell's. I managed to bump off with a few of the girls whilst Nobby came out with a myriad of excuses to put a girl off the hunt when she showed an interest.

The first week was a bit intimidating because the action on the games was heavy. I remember on the first night some geezer walking up to the roulette table upon which I was dealing. Whilst the ball was spinning, he threw over a wad of cash and shouted, "Seventeen to the maximum, six to the quarter maximum and the change on low numbers please." I froze, I had never heard of such a bet before. I was about to scream, "Help!" when the inspector watching my game ran off a total cash amount the player owed and told me to put a marker on the wheel. "You will need to learn all maximums and their divisions. The action here is similar to London. Within a few months you'll know these bets off by heart, and you'll be placing them on the layout before the ball drops," said the inspector. "Yes, sir," I replied meekly. To be honest I was actually embarrassed because we'd never been taught this sort of stuff back in Birmingham. I thought I'd learnt a lot about casinos in the UK, however, none of them I'd worked in had players making wagers such as those. Sun City was the big time in the casino world and you had to know your shit. The action in the casino was unbelievable, huge amounts of money were been wagered in every direction you cared to look. The atmosphere in the joint was electric too; finally I thought, this is what casinos should be really like. After a couple of months of adjusting to the action we were beginning to find our feet and settle into the madness of Sun City.

Nobby and me met some great lads working in Africa and one we befriended was a geezer called CCD, and he owned a Volkswagen Beetle. "You boys can us my motor on your days off if you like and go and ponce around the game reserve," said CCD.

"What fucking game reserve?" I asked.

"You're telling me you've been in Sun City nearly three months and you had no idea there is game-park next door?" he replied. Me and Nobby had only just managed to find our way around the huge complex and we had no idea there was a big fuck off game reserve next door. On our next days off, we reminded CCD of his offer, grabbed the keys from his hand and went bouncing down the road towards the Pilannesburg National Park. This is one of the smallest game reserves in the whole of Africa, yet it is roughly the size of Wales. Once we entered the park all the jazz of Sun City disappeared and now there was just endless Savannah's and various beasts dotted on the horizon. If you used your imagination you could be looking deeply into the past because nothing had really changed here since the beginning of time, well maybe not but you see what I mean.

Bob had come with us for our little excursion and he seemed to be in his natural element within the park. He

49

was banging on about hunting back in England all day long. "Where the fuck have you been hunting in Brum then?" asked Nobby.

"I used to work on a farm shovelling shit," replied Bob.

"What? Horse shit?" asked Nobby.

"No," replied Bob.

"Cow shit?" asked Nobby.

"No," replied Bob.

"Bull shit?" asked Nobby.

"Fuck off," replied the Bob.

"Will you two give it a fucking rest! You're both talking bollocks! Hold on a minute though Bob. What as shovelling shit got to do with fucking hunting?" I asked.

"Before I'd learnt the art of hunting on the various farms I worked at, I had to start at the bottom," replied Bob.

Nobby started laughing and said, "Yeah... see I was right all along then! You're taking out of your fucking arse!"

I started laughing too and glanced into the rear-view mirror to see Bob pulling his face. Nobby realized we'd caught the Bob red-handed telling a whopper, so he tried to change tack. "Did you hear about the scam some of the dealers and inspectors tried to pull in Sun City a few years ago?" A few years previous to our arrival some of the staff along with some of the players had developed an ingenious way to scam the casino. It simply revolved around slipping a empty hollow tube over a real stack of cash chips. The clever part of the scam worked like this: a player walked up to the table and bought in for $100. The empty sleeve which looked exactly like the $5 dollar chips was slipped over the £100 chips. All stacks of chips in a casino are in twenty, so it looked like the player who bought in for a $100 was getting 20 x 5 worth of $5 dollars chips. However, because the empty sleeve had been placed over the $100 chips he actually received $2000. This scam had gone on for some considerable time until all those involved were caught. It is hard to get the exact figure the casino was scammed for, but it involved many people and the estimates of casino losses ran into millions of dollars. "Yes mate, one of the lads was telling me last night, fucking unbelievable eh?" I replied. "Yeah, what is worse some of the dealers ended up in one of the notorious South African jails, and one went mad inside," said Nobby. Fuck me, the last place you'd ever want to end up in life would be in a South African jail, especially if you were a white boy living under apartheid. "I heard the British Embassy had to step in and transfer them all back to the UK to serve the remainder of their sentences because they were getting raped and beaten mercilessly," I replied. The other two went quiet for a few minutes, "Well,you make a pact with the devil and you'll get your ring burnt," said Bob.

"That reminds me Bob. Did you turn your oven off before we came here?" Nobby and me had arranged to pick him up at his apartment and once inside the smell of pizza filled the air. Nobby ended up serving up the pizza whilst me and the Bob sank a few beers.

"You took the fucking pizza out of the oven," he said, "I hope you turned it off!"

Nobby shrugged his shoulders, "I cannot remember."

Bob started to panic, "You fucking gormless git! I hope you turned it off!"

Nobby rubbed his chin, "I think I did Bob...not to worry because the maid will have been in your place by now to clean up, and she would have noticed the thick black smoke as soon as she opened the door."

I looked around at Nobby and said, "Will you give it a fucking rest winding him up?"

Nobby shrugged his shoulders, "Who's winding him up?"

"Where is Sidall anyway? I thought he was supposed to be coming with us," I asked trying to change tack.

"Fuck knows, I seen him in the crew bar last night shit-faced and told him to be around mine this morning, but I guess he's in still in bed," replied Bob.

Dave Sidall was a biker type fella, which appealed to us immediately because we'd both had an interest in the two wheeled beasts. In fact we started our own motorcycle business just after we left school, Junction Motorcycles was the company's name. I once owned a Kawasaki Z400, which was in all honesty a pile of shite. Anyway, Nobby had found a suitable buyer for the beast and the bloke came around to my house to view the machine to strike a deal. The geezer turned up and had a look around the mean machine, "Do you mind if I start it up?" he asked.

"No mate you carry on," I replied.

The bike immediately roared into life and made a racket. "Bloody hell, it's a bit loud isn't it!" Said our prospective buyer. "No mate, it's a Z400 they're supposed to sound a bit meaty," replied Nobby.

The Bloke had no idea one of the exhausts was held on with super glue and the other had a hole. Therefore, we wrapped a bit of tape and other shit around it to try to quieten it the fuck down. Strangely enough, the bloke looked quite keen on the bike and to our amazement asked for a test ride. I ran inside the house and grabbed him a helmet and quickly informed him that it was his lucky day because the helmet was included in the sale too. Our new friend looked impressed, he jumped on the bike and asked, "Mind if I take it for a spin around the block?" My old house was on Warwards Lane, which was located at the top of the hill opposite the park. The bloke grabbed a handful of throttle and in a plume of black smoke he was off down the lane.

"Erm did you mention it had no brakes mate?" asked Nobby. "No, I thought you would have told him that when you suggested it to him in the first place," I replied. The bloke came back several minutes later looking white as a ghost. Not only were his shoes fucked, his jeans were too. I forgot to mention the rip in the seat, and since we had heavy rain the previous night all the water had came back up through the foam and soaked his arse. Needless to say, our reputations has motorcycle dealers were brought in question. But we still had a passion for the beasts and Sidall happened to like the machines too.

A few weeks previous, Sidall had been telling Nobby and me how Bob reckoned he was a motorbike racer in his youth. Nobby was in hysterics because he was the one who tried to teach the Bob to ride. He was fucking useless and nearly killed himself on his very first outing. "Let the clutch out slowly Bob, and give it a little bit of gas," Nobby said at the time. Bob was on his Honda Super Dream 250cc, which wasn't the quickest of bikes. Initially Bob did exactly what he was told, but then panicked. He grabbed a hand full of throttle and let the clutch go, which immediately made the bike lurch forward. With the front wheel off the ground and with the Bob hanging on for dear life he had lost control. Nobby, had tears in his eyes whilst he recalled what happened next. He said he'd shouted, "stop, stop! Take your hand off the throttle!" but it was too late. Bob went wobbling off across the pub car-park and crashed into a Jaguar. Several burly men came rushing out of the beer garden to see what all the commotion was about, only to see Bob rolling around on the floor. Nobby said, "The only racing Bob did was when he got up to see whose car he had hit and tried to 'race off' home. Of all all the cars he had to crash into it had to be a local gangsters. It ended up costing his mom about £10,000." Well done Bob.

I found the work in the casino easy after six months because I was now accustomed to all the action, and knew what to expect from the players. The Salon Privé – private room, in Sun City catered for the high rollers who turned up virtually every week from Israel. These junkets – all expenses paid for by the casino, were where the casino could make, or lose some serious money. The Privé was set apart from the main casino floor and nobody was allowed in unless you were on a guests list. This ensured wealthy clients could gamble in total anonymity and, without fear of being hounded by more unscrupulous clients out on the make. The table limits were considerably higher than the main gaming floor, and some of the minimum stakes on blackjack were £1000 per hand. If you were lucky enough to be sent to do a shift in here you were in for a relatively easy night because the bigger the games, the easier they are to deal. Furthermore, you actually spent most of the night doing fuck all because the players would usually turn up for an hour or so, then fuck off all night. I was in there one night bored shitless when a South African girl who ran the bingo came to my table, and whispered, "meet me in the staff boozer after work." She was a blonde girl who I had been trying it on with the previous evening to no avail. Nobby and Bob didn't seem too bothered about the women in Sun City, which is still a mystery to me to this very day. There were so many good looking women from all over the world working there: dancers, dealers, shop workers et cetera. One night I'd be rolling around with a girl out of the casino, the next a girl from the shops who originated from Lebanon. Another great thing about the Privé was the fact the casino laid on a free high class buffet and free drinks. Whatever the players did not drink or eat was left for the staff once the casino had closed. You could guarantee without fail there would always be case after case of cold beer to be drunk and, plates of delicious food to be devoured. Back in England you'd be lucky to get a free pint on New Year's Eve, and here you had it all every fucking night.

Looking back now, almost thirty years later I'm amazed how much fun we really had working at this joint. I could tell you a myriad of stories me and Nobby had winding up the Bob, and most of them were in the previous editions of this book; however, I have since deleted most of them with this update because after finally reading what I had written it was a bit unfair on the poor fellow. The time Nobby done a huge shit in his toilet, the time we nearly fucked off and left him in the game reserve, the time we put a dead snake in his bed and the unfortunate episode in the pool are no more. Sorry about that, but it had to be done.

One extraordinary episode which I have decided to keep is the time when me, Nobby, Sidall and the Bob got chased by baboons up in the hills of Sun City. So without further a do, here goes. One bright sunny day we decided to ponce off up into the hills of Sun City because there was a stone age village at the top. After reaching this incredibly preserved site and after spending a good few hours at the summit, we decided to head back down the disused road to the sanctuary of Sun City before the African Sun plunged us into darkness. None of us fancied been stuck up here in the dark, fuck knows what might be lurking in the bushes. Half way down the path, we suddenly came across a troop of baboons whom were also on the path. All of us stopped and Sidall piped up, "Oi you lot, what we going to do about those fuckers?"

"Let's just walk towards them and I'm sure that will frighten them off," answered Nobby. Bob and I were a bit sceptical about walking straight at the furry twats because they looked intimidating. The baboons actually looked pleased they'd finally caught four humans up in their natural home and started making a racket. They had good reason to be hostile in retrospective, because they were treated like vermin in the complex itself. Whenever a troop of the fuckers tuned up in the middle of the night all pandemonium would break loose. You could be in bed and all you would hear were the local security guards screaming and shouting in their native tongues followed by gunshots. Anyway, as we all carried on walking towards them, it soon became apparent that they were not going to move out of the way for us. On the contrary, our continued approach seemed to agitate them into a defensive stance that looked and sounded very, very threatening. "Erm Nobby, I think we should try a different approach mate," said the Bob.

"I agree, I think we should turn around and fuck off back up the hill. There must be at least thirty of the furry bastards and there are only four of us," I replied. "Bollocks to that! I'm not going back up there! It will be dark in half an hour and then we will be really screwed, let's show them we mean business. Everybody pick up some rocks and we'll charge the fuckers!" replied Sidall. "Yeah," Bob and Nobby together. We all agreed and picked up rocks from the side of the road and then Nobby gave the count, "Right lads after three, we charge! One, two, three, charge!" shouted Nobby. We all let out an almighty roar and went charging towards are foe. Churchill would have been proud of us. As we got closer and closer we soon realized that the baboons were not playing cricket. They displayed a remarkable contempt for our haphazard approach and they decided to play us at our own game. Hitler would have been proud of them. The furry fuckers all began picking up rocks and they started to charge us! The scene was like Dunkirk all over again. Obviously, this tactical manoeuvre by the enemy stopped our front line offensive in its tracks. We all consulted with British intelligence - which happened to be Nobby, and he informed us all of our next movements. "Fucking leg it!" he screamed. Of course, we were not actually retreating, we were advancing in the other direction! We all ran through the bush and down the hillside toward Sun City with the enemy in hot pursuit, it was crazy man. Rocks were whizzing past our heads as we reached the sanctuary of the complex out of breath and feeling lucky to be alive. I then realized that Sidall was still missing in action. Sidall was gangly looking geezer at the best of times. After a few seconds, most of the boys joined up together and we were all concerned about the whereabouts of Sidall.

"I hope those fuckers ain't got him," shouted Nobby.

"Yeah, the bastards might take him into captivity and torture him," replied the Bob.

Sidall came bounding out the bushes a few seconds later and just as he reached the sanctuary of the complex, a big 'fuck off' rock hit him right on the head. Siddal struggled to his feet and we all begun laughing. His glasses were half on his face and half off with one of the lenses cracked, his hair looked like it had been in a wind tunnel and he had half the African bush protruding from possible part of his torso. Further, poor old Sidall had to go and see the doctor because of a nasty bite on his arse.

I didn't actually stay in Sun City for too long because I resigned over a fucking cat. Yes, you read that right a fucking cat. Nobby and me asked if we could move to an apartment down by the pool because the two lads in there were fucking off back to the UK for their vacation. The lads who were moving out had a kitten, and the furry little bastard had pissed all over the carpets. Now, if anybody knows what cat piss smells like you'll know what I am talking about here; it absolutely fucking stank. Because it's always hot in South Africa, it seemed to make the stench ten timed worse. Anyway, we went to maintenance and asked them for a new carpet. The geezer in the joint said he'd be around to fit it within 24 hours. A few days later the maintenance fella still hadn't turned up so I called the maintenance department, "Oi, when is this carpet coming mate? We've already taken the old one out to save your boys the trouble," I said. An hour later another geezer came around and asked who had given us permission to take the old carpet out. We explained that since the people in the maintenance office promised that they would deliver and lay the new carpet, the previous day, I thought I would save them the trouble. The man informed me that there was no record of either of us calling maintenance and furthermore, we would have to replace the old carpet, or buy a new one since we had no authority to undertake such things.

"You have got to be taking the fucking piss haven't you?" I said. "Like I said, there is no record of you requesting a new carpet, and you have no authority to take the company's property without permission."

I looked at the bloke through squinted eyes, "OK sunshine, I have had enough of this. I will see our boss in the casino later and he can sort it out with you." That night I went to see the GM and explained to him the situation. He did not give a shit. In fact, he backed up the maintenance geezer, whom happened to be a South African white boy. He then said, "You and Paul will have to pay for the carpet." Stunned, I told him to fuck off and resigned there and then. There is no way in this world I'm going to work for anybody whom doesn't trust his own staff on an issue concerning a fucking carpet. After all, we deal games where hundreds of thousands of dollars changed hands virtually every night and he couldn't trust us over a poxy carpet? Nah mate, I do not play those sorts of games. Nobby was shocked; many people in Sun City were too. I would not back down though and it was time to leave. The funny thing is a few months later, I had a phone call from Nobby explaining that the geezer whom came around to the apartment making noise about the carpet was actually on the fiddle. He had been selling the company's stock and cooking the books. He wanted Nobby and I to pay for the carpet, which he had already sold, what a wanker.

ATLANTIC ASSOCIATES

Before I had left Sun City a fellow named Dean Evans had told me about working on the ships out of Miami. "Windmill, you're mad going back to England, but I fully understand why you're leaving you stubborn bastard. Get your arse down to London and see Lesley Lees, she will sort you out," he said at the time. Before that, I fucked off to the Canary Islands for a few months to chill out, which was a great little adventure because I was working in a couple of nightclubs, and managed to bang a Spanish girl who couldn't even speak a word of English. A few weeks after I'd arrived home from the Canaries, I took Deans advice and called Atlantic Associates who were advertising for dealers in Florida. I went down to London and met a woman named Janet Stephens for the initial interviews and was offered a job immediately. She said, "Your placement will arrive in the post within the next month. Be ready to go and welcome to Atlantic Associates." A few weeks later I was on the plane again, this time flying to Miami to join a ship called The Tropicana. Once in Miami, I caught a cab across to South Beach to our apartments, which were actually in a hotel called the Royal Palm on Collins Avenue. I arrived at the hotel late in the afternoon, the place had seen better days, but it backed onto Miami Beach itself, which was the jewel in the crown as far as I was concerned. The hotel was deserted so I presumed all the casino crew were out on the sea working the evening shift. The room I was staying in was on the second floor, overlooking the pool. There was a picture of a geezer with glasses on the wall with the words, 'Billy I love you,' written below. "Fucking hell, don't tell me I have come all this way to be roomed with a bellend," I thought. Thing is, when I finally met Billy - who was a Turkish fellow, he was the salt of the earth and as mad as a box of frogs. Miami Beach was a lot different in the very late eighties to what it is nowadays. Most of the hotels on the drive catered for elderly Jews who had come down to Miami for their final days, "God's waiting room," as one fella liked to call the place. Today Miami Beach is renowned world wide for its vibrant nightlife, back then it really wasn't much at all.

It was a Friday night, the drive down to the port of Miami and the ship took a mere ten minutes. Miami at night is just as impressive as it is by day. The mentally of the people here seemed different to those in England, many teenagers in the UK where out scowling and trying to look like they were cool. You know the sort, two bob cunts on the dole smoking shit all day long in their dirty grey tracksuits. Here in Miami, they were smiling and wanted to be your best friend. I suppose I was being pretty naivé because we were located slap bang in the middle of the tourist suburbs. I wasn't sure if all areas of Miami would be so accommodating. In fact I knew they wouldn't because there are quite a few films explaining the frightening world of Miami's underground and, the destruction it has caused. Miami is actually built on cocaine money, or so the saying goes.

The Tropicana was a strange ship; well you could not really class her as such. In her previous years she had been a cross channel ferry between Harwich in England and the ports of northern Europe. She weighed in at only 6,500 tons. I did not I know anything about ships at this time, in fact it was the first boat of any considerable size that I had ever ventured upon and I initially found the labyrinth of corridors below decks overwhelming. I was forever getting lost. The schedule the casino staff worked was easy, we would be doing 'nowhere' cruises. This basically meant that we weren't actually going anywhere in particular, just a cruise out of Miami Beach on the ocean waves for a few hours. On the other days, we sailed to an Island in the Bahamas called Bimini. This was brilliant because it was only two and a half hours from Miami, and we would have five hours on the island. My newfound mate on the ship, Nigel Green and me fucked off to the beach with some of the girls.

The beach on Bimini, along with the weather was superb. We found a quiet spot and discussed our time on the ship, "Well I've just joined, so know fuck all about ships to be honest, but I already know I'm going to enjoy my time here," I said. "You're mistaken if you think that thing is a fucking ship mate," replied Greeny.
"What do you mean?" I asked.
"Well, for starters it is not actually a ship as such but an old cross channel ferry."
At that moment some dude came along the beach selling booze from a cooler he had on his fucking head.
"Rum punch?" he asked?
"Don't mind if I do," I replied.
"Now this is fucking cool, getting served booze on the beach. Where does this happen in the UK?" I said whilst supping on the concoction which, may I add was awfully strong.
"So you was saying that the Tropicana isn't a ship then? Well excuse me if I sound stupid, but what the fuck is it then?" I asked.
"A fucking tug boat mate, wait until we go to the capital Nassau and you'll see some real ships," replied Greeny

whilst laughing. We went into the the pristine water which was as warm as a bath. The colours in the water were stunning. I had never seen such clear water before, even in Cornwall where the gulf stream brings up the water from the Caribbean isn't this clear. Three hours later I was back onboard burnt to a toast; the sun here is fiercely hot. Those first three weeks went incredibly quickly and being in Miami was pure bliss. Unfortunately, this didn't last too long because the company relocated the ship to Cape Canaveral some 200+ miles up the coast.

The hotel in Canaveral - which was out in the middle of nowhere, had its own lake and it even had a few resident alligators living in the lake outside. The place was dull compared to Miami, however, me and Mr. Green managed to get ourselves into a bit of bother because one night we got wankered in the bar and decided to go skinny dipping in the lake. The next morning somebody was shaking me violently. The casino manager was not very happy to find me curled up on a bench overlooking the lake, or to find Nigel fast asleep by the water's edge. "You pair of fucking idiots!" he raged. "Do you know how dangerous it is for you to be sleeping here? Do you? That lake has several large gators in it, now get to your rooms and I will speak to you both later."
We were banned from the bar for a week and we were also prohibited from going anywhere near the lake indefinitely, which was probably a good thing.

The ship relocated again, this time to Tampa Bay, which was also a riot. Some New Yorkers' owned the hotel this time and they were all cool. One day the ship had gone out on a gambling cruise in rough weather. I was off and consequentially missed all the fun. Apparently, it was that rough the coast guard informed the Tropicana not to sail, but the captain wasn't having any of that! He went out anyway, but soon discovered that it was indeed too rough. Some of the casino crew were crying with laughter when they told me what happened next. "The fucking captain came on the tannoy and said, "Ladies and gentleman the weather has worsened since we left the dock, and therefore I will be turning the ship around. Please sit down in the lounges whilst we make this turn." "The ship then turned and was immediately hit by this massive wave," said Nigel.

"What happened next?" I asked all bright eyed and bushy tailed, eager to find out more.

"The passengers who were standing on the port side of the boat ended up on the starboard side, all stuck to the fucking windows."

"You've got to be joking?" I replied, smiling.

"No I ain't, and it got worse, in the casino, all the old gits that were sitting at the tables ended up on the floor, with the tables and the dealers on top of them."

By this time I was howling too, I missed all the fun! What a pisser. The captain received the bullet because a load of the old duffers needed hospital treatment and the ship had suffered substantially damage. America is a: sue, sue and sue em some more country. Any chance they get to put in claim, they will take it. I would find this out much later with a hilarious episode on another ship.

I soon found out that friendships could forged one day, only to discover that somebody would be transferred the day after. That somebody, this time, was me. They needed a dealer on a ship called The Majestic. It was not a gambling ship, but a three and four day cruise ship. I was a bit shocked about going because I only had five weeks left on my contract, but all the other old sea dogs informed me that this was common practice with the company, they wanted to see if I was suitable to work on their cruisers, so I was naturally off to the smallest ship in the fleet. The Majestic looked gigantic compared to the Tropicana; this ship had been designed for world cruising, and was known as the '*Big Red Boat.*' This probably had something to do with the fact that it was painted bright red. I must admit it was fine looking inside compared to the Tropicana, which had probably seen better days.

I had only been on the ship two days when a purser from New York was dragging me around her cabin after a night in the crew bar. I really was starting to get to grips with this ship life; it was a basically a free for all. My cabin mate on here was geezer from Manchester in England, his name was Tony Joy, and he was a cashier. The Majestic was going to be a riot for me and Tony during my very brief spell working on her because

ultimately I would be sent home early and with that, all
hope of working on cruise liners with AA in the future
evaporated. The actual casino onboard the Majestic was a
lot smaller than that of the Tropicana, less than half the
table games. Even so, the crew onboard were all decent
enough and we all got along great! One of the dealers
named Martin Kelly was hilarious, he used to take his
shoes off and have them protruding from behind a curtain
right next to the dice table. This used to freak some of the
players out because they thought somebody was hiding.
One guy spotted them and kept glancing perplexed, trying
to figure out what was going on.

Martin said to him, "The man's wife had caught him with
a female passenger, and she was hunting for him around
the vessel with a machete."

"No shit?" replied the bloke.

The officers were mostly Greeks and they resented most
of the casino staff because we had a reputation of partying
and getting drunk all the time. Well what else do expect
us to do? We have one of the best jobs onboard, we only
work when the ship is sailing and we had no other duties.
I firmly believed that in reality the Greeks were slightly
jealous. Anyway, Tony and I managed to rob some pyrate
gear off some of the cast in the show. After another night
in the crew bar, we would dress up in our clobber and raid
all the female cabins. We acquired the tag, 'The Pyrates
of Tween Deck.' It was hilarious, we would be shit-faced
and just steam into a cabin, anybodies cabin and start

shagging. When I say shagging, I mean we would be shagging anything: the cupboard, the television, the door, and even the girls' legs. We would have running battles with the women in their own cabins has they tried in vain to throw us out. If we managed to 'board' their beds, they were in deep trouble. After one evening's shenanigans, one of the Greek security officers caught us in the corridor shagging one of the laundry carts.

"Oi, you two pyrates stop!" he shouted, and that was it, it was like a wild goose chase around the corridors with Socrates frantically radioing for back up. This carried on for the next few weeks and me and Tony had become legends on the ship. The poor old Greeks had no idea it was us, they suspected, but they could not prove anything.

"Fucking hell Tony, guess what son? We have the next cruise off because we have a load of Christian bible bashers onboard!" I said to Tony.

"You're fucking joking? No way, ah, this is going to be fun," he replied. So off we went banging on the casts door again to find out what goodies they might have for us. Would you believe they actually had a devils costume, now things were really going to heat up.

The first night of the cruise we decided to keep a low profile because we knew the officers would have extra security watching the casino cabins. They knew we were off, and they knew that this was their best chance of actually catching us in the act. The next day we were on the company's private island in the Abaco Islands.

The island was quality compared with either Bimini or Freeport. Tiny and with no inhabitants whatsoever, the place was also spotlessly clean. One of the divers used to let us use his jet ski all day whilst he was poncing about under the waves. It was of the older types that you actually stood up on, much more fun than those modern things. We spent most the day speeding round the Abaco's countless sand banks and island inlets. The ship would stay overnight, but all the passengers had to be back onboard by 9pm, this is where the real fun began and the divers where going to let Tony and me in on the action. "You guys wanna stay behind and have a bit of fun with the sharks?" said Toby, an American kid from Florida. "Absolutely," Tony roared enthusiastically. The divers would snorkel out and catch a few fishes, then put them on a hook, which was attached to a big fuck off thick rope. They'd just threw it into the water and waited. "Don't either of you go into the water," Toby instructed us. "Why, is jaws lurking or something?" I asked. "You'll see," said Toby whilst chucking to himself.

Within minutes there were sharks everywhere, it really was surreal, "Oi Windmill look at that!" screamed Tony. I could not believe my eyes for a second, but when the divers started having a tug of war with a shark, I suddenly realized what was happening. It took four grown men to pull a five-foot shark out of the water; the creature was thrashing about like a lunatic, in the surf and on the beach. One of Toby's mates jumped directly onto the sharks back. It was crazy man, the sharks head was moving side to side in slow motion trying to bite the fucker. Tony and I were laughing our heads off, it is not every day you see some geezer trying to wrestle with a shark on a beach now is it? Eventually once the shark was tiring; one of the other divers grabbed it by the tail and started swinging it around. When he had enough speed up, he launched the thing back into the water. The shark was obviously stunned for a moment then casually swam off as if nothing had happened.

Later that night in the crew bar we were all having a good old giggle about it and at some point during the evening, me and Tony made our way below decks to continue with or plans to terrorize the crew. I think we had drunk more than normal, because we ended up in the passenger cabin areas. I was dressed has a pyrate and Tony was dressed has the devil, he even had a three forked prong! We found a suitable door, located by one of the crew stairwells, "Right after three, we knock on the door and go steaming into the cabin," I said.
Tony could hardly stand up, he was in hysterics.
"OK, OK, I'm ready, one, two..."
Then all pandemonium broke loose, we were banging on the door and making such a racket that even Satan himself would have been proud of us. Sure enough, some geezer opened the door to see what all the commotion was about. You should have seen the look on his face when the Devil and his three-forked prong and a Pyrate confronted him

with his sword at the ready.

"Out Satan out; be gone from here!" Yelled the Christian bloke. After some pushing and shoving the man eventually managed to close the bloody door, Tony and I ended up on the floor howling with laughter.

"Come on Tony, come on son, we have to get back below decks; Socrates, Plato and Aristotle will be up here any minute now," I said.

"You...you fucking go mate. My ribs are killing me!" replied Tony.

However, he soon focused because right at the other end of the corridor two of the officers suddenly appeared.

"Stop, pyrates!" they screamed half-heartedly.

I was beginning to wonder if they enjoyed chasing us pair of twats around the ship as we enjoyed running away from them. I suppose it made for an exciting night for them, and broke up the monotony of prowling deserted passageways all night. This time we made a fatal error in judgement though, instead of heading below decks, we jumped into a passenger elevator and made our way up. The elevator stopped on the 7th floor and we were now in a big world of shit. We were now on passenger floors and there were officers everywhere.

"Pyrates, stop!" one of them yelled and this time when we made a run for it, we went in different directions.

I do not know what happened next even to this day.

I could not remember falling down the main staircase, but I remember a female passenger waking me up. Fuck knows how I had managed to get into that position either; I was upside down lying on my back.

"Are you OK, sir?" asked the concerned voice of the passenger.

"Where am I?" I replied, before getting up and legging it down the stairs again. I managed to get as far as the crew quarters when two beefy Greeks grabbed hold of me, "Ah Ahh! Finally pyrate we caught you," said one of the smiling Greeks.

"It's a fair cop boys," I slurred. The ship actually went to the capital of the Bahamas that night because they were expecting rough weather. Nassau is a bustling city compared to the other islands. I remember sitting on the back deck looking over the harbour, something about the place was going to play apart in my future but I just did not know what that was at the time. By the time we arrived in Canaveral, one of the people from office in Miami was waiting for me on the dock. Subsequently I was to be sent home early on vacation. Strangely, they did not fire me. Before I signed of one of the girls shaved one of my fucking eyebrows off. I looked like a right twat in Miami airport everybody was pointing and laughing.

In hindsight the Majestic was an absolute pleasure to work upon, even though we were out of order the staff and crew were superb.

LONDON CALLING

It was great getting back to England, everything was happening around this time, the music was superb and everybody was chilled out - even the women. I grew up in Selly Oak, it's a suburb in the south-west of the City of Birmingham. After spending the first day with the family, Nobby turned up. "Fucking hell Windmill you've put a bit of timber on ain't you." I was not going argue with him because his description was accurate, I could just about see my feet. "You can talk lard arse! Anyway, when are you applying for the ships?" I asked.

"You're coming to London with me next week,' he replied.

"Why, what's happening down there?"

"Well I have an interview with Atlantic Associates."

He had received conformation in the post and had been accepted for the preliminary interviews in London.

A few weeks later we snaked our way across south-west London towards the Embassy Hotel. Upon arrival, I had a quiet word with him in the lobby. "What ever you do Nobby, do not tell the boss I'm here, do you understand me?" I said.

"Why? You in some sort of trouble," he asked.

"Not really, but she might give me a mouthful if she knows I'm here. I was talking to some of the boys in Miami and I've already got a reputation for being a bit wild," I replied.

"OK no problem," Nobby answered with a big grin on his

face. There were about thirty people awaiting an interview on the seventh floor of the hotel, a mixture of boys and girls all looking nervous about meeting the legendary Lesley Lees. Eventually the boss opened the door, greeted everybody outside and instructed all to follow her into the room. I put my head down and did not utter a word. "Are you not here for an interview too?" She asked. "No, no I'm here with my friend. I'm just waiting for him thank you," I replied whilst trying to hide my face. All seemed to go smoothly because by the time I lifted my head the corridor was empty and the door into the interview room was just closing behind them all.
I could hear muffled voices coming from behind the door and several minutes later, I suddenly heard a woman shriek, "What!" and before I knew what was happening the door flew open and the boss was dragging me into the room by the ear. Nobby the paper hat, had dropped me in the shit.

"This is a perfect example of what you must not do whilst working for the company onboard our ships," she said in a loud clear voice, "This young man thinks it's very clever to sleep next to a pool infested with alligators whilst drunk. He also thinks it's OK to run riot around another ships quarters dressed as a pirate whilst shagging anything in his sight, including laundry carts!"
The room burst out laughing and I went as red as a tomato. I could not believe just how much information she had concerning her staff, there were hundreds of us

working for her and she knew exactly what we all had been doing. She was good, very fucking good.

The boss finished her little speech about the dos and don't s onboard the ships and banished me from the room. As I was leaving, she gave me a heartening smile and said she would be in touch shortly. Nobby and I went on the lash in London after that, he said the interview went very well and he said she had spoken highly of me after I had left the room. "Phew," I said, "for a minute she was going to hand me a box of cards with just the 9, 10, Jack inside."

A week later, she called from her office in Miami and said that I would be signing on a ship called The Discovery the following week. I had heard all about the Discovery, it was a notorious gambling boat out of Fort Lauderdale in Florida. The ship was also the place where they sent all the bad boys of the company. People told me it was hard work but all the dealers lived together in apartment blocks called Harbor House, which was a stones thrown from the port. I had heard via other shipmates working for the company, that the place was an absolute riot.

FRONTLINE WINNER

I have cut this, and subsequent chapters right down from the original book, otherwise it would be a book in its own right explaining all the shenanigans going on in Lauderdale. I have also cut out many of the the characters out simply because I cannot remember all the people I worked with last month, never mind 25yrs ago, and kept receiving reminders from people on social media about this that and the other. Therefore, I have condensed them to a few paragraphs.

The plane touched down in Miami at around 5pm in the afternoon, it was great to be back in Florida. Fort Lauderdale was located roughly 20 miles north of Miami, and was considered a wealthy city on the east coast. I caught the super shuttle and arrived at the infamous Harbor House at around 7pm. The place was practically deserted; I figured everybody must have been at work. The room was fairy spacious and it had a large kitchen with a huge fridge filled with nice cold beers. I would be rooming with two other blokes because there were three beds in the apartment. Rumour had it that Harbor House had forty plus casino staff living within its walls at any given time. By ten o'clock, a huge old school bus had turned up and a load of nutters came running from its doors. Suddenly the door of my apartment flew open and two geezers came steaming in, one was an Australian by the name of Rodney Pike and the other was an old hippy from Manchester called Nick. The three of us hit it off immediately; they also showed me the ropes concerning everything to do with Harbor House and the surrounding vicinity. My schedule dictated that I'd be at work the following morning and we had to be at the ship, which was located five minutes away, at 10am.
The Discovery looked to be a fair sized ship compared to

the last two I had worked on, but once inside the vessel itself I was amazed at the size of the casino. The ship been designed for one purpose and one purpose only, gambling. The casino was split on two decks, it had three dice tables, shit loads of blackjacks and several roulette tables. A new game called Caribbean Stud Poker was also on the ship. Now most dealers could not believe people actually played this game because it's plainly ridiculous; however, I love poker! The reason will be explained a little later.

All the casino crew were on the back deck talking shit, I recognized a few of the gang from other ships, so this always helps. Somebody stood up and shouted, "Right you lot, time to go," and everybody made their way to the casino, most of them moaning. I could not believe my eyes when we all went into the pit, "Fucking hell, ah Ahh!" I screamed. 90% of the management team were from Birmingham and I knew them all. Stuart Reading from the Rainbow said to me, "Listen Windmill, the boss has already filled me in with regards to your misbehaving on the other ships and she had instructed me to keep a close eye on you!" Whatever did she mean?

A few weeks later we – the casino staff, had a huge fight at the City Limits nightclub in Fort Lauderdale one evening, and the name windmill really began to make sense to all the dealers on the fucking ship. This was a seedy club where all the dealers and so forth would congregate after another legendary hangout for the casino crew called the Raw Bar had closed for the evening. I remember being in the club with some of the lads drinking beers when all hell broke loose. The clubs bouncers threw out one of the dealers for being drunk. Outside a punch up had developed, the fracas had escalated and it soon turned into a running battle outside the club between the Americans and the Brits. Fists and boots were flying in from all over the place and there must have been at least thirty people scrapping outside. As soon as I entered the ruckus some bouncer sprayed me in the eyes with mace. Now, this shit stings like fuck and I couldn't see fuck all. I was rubbing my eyes whilst hearing the thud, thud, thud of punches and boots with the occasional scream as some cunt was kicked in the bollocks. There was only one thing left to do, grin and bare the the pain in my eyes and start fucking wind milling. The only problem with this tactic is you cannot see who you're chinning. Later I heard I hit more of our lads than the Americans.

The English contingent in Fort Lauderdale were becoming so popular with the locals that they opened a bar purely for us called The Crucible, which was located a stones throw from our other favourite hangout, the Raw Bar. We were not the only ship to dock on the causeway, another gambling ship named The Scandinavian Dawn operated out of the harbour too. This was another legendary ship – of which I will get to latter, that made Lauderdale such an exciting place to be in the 1990s.

I passed my driving test in Fort Lauderdale, all for the princely sum of $20. The test proved to be easier than you could possibly imagine. All I did was drive a few hundred yards down a road, hit the brakes, do a three-point turn, and then head back to the test centre.

"Well, how did I do?" I asked the instructor.

"You passed Sir," replied the woman.

A few weeks later Nick and I fucked off down to Miami on our days off in a car I had hired. We departed Lauderdale at 11 am, and by 2-30 pm, I had a huge accident on Collins Avenue with a BMW, which caused £10,000 worth of damage. The driver of the BMW happened to be a female lawyer and the copper who turned up happened to be one of her mates. The argument between the four of us raged for well over an hour.

"How on earth could she only have been doing 30 mph, skid 50 feet over an intersection, and then write-off another car?" I asked the copper.

The copper said I had swerved across the inside lane and made her press the gas instead of the brake. I could not stop laughing, what a fucking joke.

"Well what the hell is she doing overtaking on the inside lane anyway?" I replied.

Anyway, I eventually received the ticket, which meant that it was entirely my fault. The lawyer woman wasted no time getting her priorities sorted out and within a week of the accident, a letter from her law firm arrived in the post, demanding that I compensated her for all the injuries

she had never received. These included: whiplash, loss of memory, dizziness and naturally the damage to her car.
I was telling one of the regular players on the ship about my little episode and he informed me that he too was a lawyer. "I will take care of it for you."
What a geezer! I never heard from the woman again. You gotta love the Americans.

I mostly dealt dice on the Discovery and we had some quality dealers man. The only problem with working the dice game for Atlantic Associates was that there was no Come Bar – for those who do not understand the dice game this a method of betting, on the layouts.
This meant that all the action consisted of place bets and the dice were not stopping for anybody. If you were not fast enough on the game, you where benched - aka thrown off the game and sent back to blackjack tables with your tail between your legs. Dice was always the best game, and still is the best to deal. Even the most reserved of people could be whipped up into frenzy around a dice game in full flow. This was its core beauty because everybody around the dice table is betting on one person to either win or lose them money. It could be like a real fucking drama around these tables, people swearing and shouting, or kissing and hugging. There is no substitute for the game in any casino, anywhere in the world.
"Winner, Winner Front Line Winner," shouted the stick-man – the bloke who passes the dice to a player to throw, and this girl lifted up her top to reveal the biggest pair of

bumpers in Florida. She was bouncing them around whilst screaming and shouting. Welcome to the zany world of the dice dealers.

"Windmill you coming down City Limits with the lads tonight," asked Rodney. "Yes, of course," I replied. Later that evening and definitely worse for the wear, I managed to pull some girl from Manchester of all places, and what happened later that night became the butt of jokes back on the ship the following day. I cannot really remember what happened because I was wasted, however, my room-mate Nick back at Harbor House said, "The girl would not stop farting whilst you were riding her. So you put some chewing gum up her arse to plug the hole." "You're fucking joking?" I replied in shock.
A few days later in the casino I timidly asked the girl in question whether it was true.
"You know how dealers gossip Windmill. Thing's have been blown out of all proportion," she replied.

The ships were brilliant during this era because if you were posted to one of the many gambling ships in Florida, you then had the option to live on land. Also, if you worked on one of the cruise ships they were a lot smaller and spent a lot longer in ports than they do these days. Thus, it really was the golden age for any casino staff who worked on ships in the late 1980s early 1990s.

BENNY'S HOPPING

After serving eight months on Discovery, I took my vacation back in good ole blighty and chilled the fuck out for a few months. The office in Miami called unexpectedly, and said they desperately needed a dice dealer to join the Scandinavian Dawn out of Fort Lauderdale immediately. "Sound, send the tickets over and I'll be on my way," I replied.

"One more thing Windmill, there are some new hires joining. Meet them at Heathrow and take care of them. Oh, and please try and turn up sober in Miami," said the woman. A few days later, I met the new lads at Heathrow and we awaited information on the flight over to Miami. A British Airways representative announced over the intercom, "British Airways would like to inform all passengers on flight BA 323 to Miami that the airline is offering any customer £200 if they would take either a later flight this evening, or £200 and hotel accommodation if they would kindly take the flight tomorrow morning. Unfortunately, this is due to a technical issue with the companies booking facilities and flight BA 323 has been overbooked. Would any interested individuals please make your way to the desk, thank you for your cooperation."

"£200 quid? a night in London, in a hotel, I'll have a bit of that!" I roared and went rushing up to the desk. I called the new hires over and asked them what they were going to do. They were obviously very sceptical about my cunning plan and because they were new, they didn't want to take the piss on their first day on the job. They would soon learn, it is a dog eat dog world, get what you fucking well can. They informed me that they were sticking to the original itinerary that the company had given them and they hoped to see me in Miami in the future. "Bon voyage boys!" I said with a glint in my eye. I was already planning my night out in London. "I will fuck off down the West End for a night on the tiles, and maybe I'll even pull an old boiler for the night," I muttered under my breath. Well this was the plan I had conjured up in my devious mind. My sneaky plans were brought crashing down to Earth when I eventually reached the desk though. All the people in front of me had taken up the allocation of freebies, in fact some American geezer managed to get the last hotel room on offer. He had a big grin on his face and turned to his buddy and said, "Wow this is so fucking cool dude! British hospitality rocks man! They've put us in a hotel in the west end and they've given us £200 to party with! Lets go out on the piss! We might even pull some more of those English slappers!" I stood at the desk inwardly smiling whilst shaking my head; that could have been me, wankers! "I'm sorry to inform you S…,"

"I know, I know, they were the last tickets."

I had interrupted the representative in mid sentence.

"Sir not to worry. The passengers whom were kind enough to offer up their seats will be upgraded to club class." The smile came back to my face immediately, "I will take it!" I roared.

Flying across the Atlantic in club class was exquisite, no plastic knives and forks in here, no plastic plates or cups and the seats were real imitation leather. I was in heaven. Not only that, the legroom was amazing compared to what the 'peasants' sitting down at the back in steerage had. We had been in the air for about thirty minutes, when one of the trolley dollies came around pouring champagne into our real champagne glasses. I instinctively looked aft into the steerage cabin to see the two new hires squashed together in the middle isle, trying desperately not to invade anybody else's space, "wankers!" I uttered whilst sipping on the bucks-fizz.

As usual, we arrived in Miami mid afternoon and went through customs. The majority of crew hated going through customs in Miami because they could be a real pain in the arse. It reminds me of when I arrived from the UK with another dealer and a bloke called Mark Ranford during the first Gulf War. There was hardly anybody on the plane because people were afraid of flying. There were only something like 170 people on a Jumbo Jet that could hold 550. Anyway to cut a long story short, the air-hostesses liked us because we were in the casino industry and they plied us with drinks. By the time we reached Miami we were all wankered and what happened at customs was hilarious. This Ranford bloke wasn't actually coming with us to Lauderdale, he was working at the

Princess casino in Freeport Bahamas, but I knew him from the days of the Rainbow. He had this leather briefcase with him and at the customs desk whilst opening it to find his passport he somehow managed to spill the contents all over the custom guys desk. The customs bloke kicked off and Ranford called him a "cunt." The next thing you know lights are flashing and a load of security blokes came rushing out of an office and carried him of kicking and screaming. I could not stop laughing, and heard later he'd actually been put on the first flight back home.

We finally arrived in Lauderdale at Eight pm. The ship was not in the port, I figured the thing either was on a cruise or had sunk. So given the fact that it probably would not be in the harbour for several more hours, I took the initiative and took the new hires to the Raw Bar. "Windmill you prat," shouted one of the dealers, "ha ha you fucker, welcome back." A few of the old faces were in the bar and it was good to see them. "Don't you get too cosy with Windmill. He'll get you into all sorts of trouble," shouted another. "Bollocks," I replied with a smile on my face. We all spent the next few hours having some drinks and tucking into the fabulous seafood that the Raw Bar also served up. We eventually made it down to the docks at two-am, wankered.

I do not remember getting to my cabin; in fact I could not remember anything. I awoke at about 10am because somebody was banging away on my cabin door.

"Oi Windmill, open the fucking door!" said a muffled voice. I eventually opened the door to find a few of the nutters I had worked with on the Discovery.

"No, no, not you lot,' I was laughing, I could just not believe what I was seeing.

"What time we sailing?" I asked whilst shaking my head and smiling. "In twenty minutes, get your uniform on and we'll see you up on back deck," answered one of the boys. I eventually made my way to the back deck to find all the boys hovering around the railings, all looking over the side. "Alright boys," I said to all of them, there were obviously a few lads on here that I had not yet met. Two geezers from Newcastle had cans of beer in their hands and they were watching the port guy untie the ships ropes. I was trying to figure out what they were up to, when one of them unexpectedly hurled the missile directly at the bloke on the dock. Fuck knows how it missed the poor chap, the can exploded upon impact feet from him. I soon got to know all the lads and ladette's in the casino, this bunch were even more crazier than the Discovery crew, I knew things were going to be wild but as yet, had no idea how wild things would actually be.

Stuart Reading was once again my manager on here and he commanded the utmost respect from all whom worked for him. His philosophy was simple; he would inform all incoming staff that they, not he, actually ran the casino and that the only time he would step in was if any of us messed up. He would also say that he expected everybody to work has a team and look out for each other. This simple statement had profound implications within the casino because Stuart also had the ability to get the right people on the right ships to work for him. His casinos always ran like clockwork, we worked hard and partied hard. Everybody knew there place. However, if you dared cross him, it was good-bye.

Everybody had their own cabin on the ship and the parties were non-stop! I was permanently on dice and it was lots of fun, until one day a new hire joined the game, it was Bundy from the Wheel in Birmingham.
I was on third base, I looked up and saw him standing there holding the fucking stick.
"What's up, you look like you've just seen a ghost?" asked the boxman.
"Which fucking idiot gave him a job? More importantly, why is he on this ship?" I answered.
Bundy had a hesitant stance about him and his brow had broken out into a sweat. He must have known the game was up before it had even begun. Immediately Bundy was benched – thrown off the game, by the boxman and within a week Stuart had him thrown off the ship, retribution had been served. One of the positive things to happen, the company finally introduced the full game by offering the come bar. The Dawn was a lot busier than the Discovery and there was a substantial amount of cash floating around the joint. Everybody and I mean everybody on the ship was a piss head. Since the entire

casino lived together at the back of the ship, all we had to do was close the fire doors and we were locked into our own little world. Down the road from the dock was a restaurant called Joe's Diner and we would all occasionally go down there for a knees up, in fact that year we held our Christmas Party in the joint. It all ended in a massive food fight because one of the lads bought a big fuck-off cake, and shoved it into one of the girls faces he did not like, "Have a bit of that you cunt," he shouted before thrusting it straight into her mush. Five minutes later, every cake in the joint had been used as ammunition during 'the battle of the bar.'

One of the funniest things I have ever witnessed on the ships was the day the Dawn announced, that it would be doing two hour gambling cruises for the Bahamians out of the Island of Freeport. Everybody on the ship was mystified by this, but it turned out to be a riot. The Bahamians aren't allowed to gamble in their country, so the idea was a good one as far as the company were concerned. The first and only gambling cruise turned into pandemonium because the Bahamians were crazy.
I think we had the entire workforce of both casinos from the island onboard. Within minutes of opening the casino doors, both crap tables were ten deep at each end, and loads of dollar bills were on the layout. I was on the stick and passed the dice to the shooter. The geezer just picked up the dice and shouted: "Mudda fuckerz!" They hit another player at the other end on the forehead and nearly

knocked him out! The whole crew were in hysterics.

"Sir, sir you cannot throw the dice like that," said one of the supervisors.

"Sorry boss, sorry," replied the shooter. I passed the dice to him again and he picked them up straight away threw them hitting the same bloke at the other end of the table in exactly the same spot on the fucking head.

The geezers were screaming, shouting and a fight soon developed. The dice crew doubled up in fits of laughter, it was hilarious. We later discovered that the players were from the rival casinos on the island, and there was bad blood between the two groups. The two hours seemed to last two fucking days and the company never made the same mistake again. Whilst in Freeport something very peculiar happened. One of the dealers went nuts and jumped off the back of the ship as we were pulling out of the harbour. One the way down to the drink, he was shouting out he was free. After they had fished him out, he received the 9 10 jack.

Things in the office were not going to plan; they were constantly coming up with excuses concerning the tip checks we received every four months. People were starting to get pissed off because not only were they fucking around with peoples wages, they were bringing in stupid rules and regulations that none of the gaming staff agreed with. Six of the dice dealers - myself included, decided it was probably a good time to change companies because we all felt that AA's days were numbered.

Therefore, we hired a mini bus and fucked off down to Miami to have table tests for a company called Tiber Trading.

Tiber had concessions for Norwegian Cruise Lines and other gambling ships based around the United States. The geezer who was in charge of operations - a bloke called David Rolls, was a good lad himself and he sent the six of us for a table test on one of his ships which was docked in the Port of Miami. The table test was easy, and Lawrence Evans and I offered employment immediately. We were issued letters of employment and were told we would be flying to San Diego the following Monday to join a ship called The Pacific Star.
This turned out to be a daily gambling ship between the States and Mexico. It was February 1992 and I had mixed feelings about leaving Atlantic. I had worked for them since 1989; I'd had some wonderful times and met some brilliant people along the way. All the same, it was time to go; this is the nature of the casino industry. Little did I know at the time, but the change to Tiber would have a massive effect towards that strange feeling I had once had in the harbour of Nassau.

ACID DAZE

San Diego is a wonderful city, very different to Lauderdale or Miami, but just as cool. The place seemed to be very affluent and you could feel the difference between the Californians and the Floridians. They definitely had different attitudes towards life; the Californians were slightly more laid back. The place had a massive Irish influence and many of the bars were 'themed' Irish drinking houses. The Pacific Star was an old bucket of a ship which was top heavy. Every time we left the harbour, you would have to hang on for dear life, on a perfectly calm sea, the thing would rock 15 degrees' or more from side to side. The boat was a nightmare. Everybody said the reason for this was because the casino was located near the top deck and the ship wasn't designed to carry all that excess weight. The casino crew all looked chilled; obviously, the Californian lifestyle had rubbed off on them. The manager was a geezer called 'Storming Spalding.' He was a giant of a man and apparently, he had a huge chopper. In fact he used to be a lumberjack before he entered the casino business and he seemed OK. The boxman seemed to be a bit of a prick though; he was a cockney fella who looked like he'd sat on a bog brush many years ago and the thing was still rammed up his rusty bullet-hole.

Lawrence and I were on the dice game whipping the punters into a frenzy, trying to earn some tips and he would be sitting there getting pissed off. As the roll progressed this would agitate the miserable git even more. The shooter had made a point of 10 and I insisted that he had a two-way hard 10 - which means the dice must roll 5 and 5 rather than 6 and 4, sure enough the dice roll 5 and 5: "*10 ,10 cock n hen, the biggest dick in Hampton Wick*

the longest willy in Piccadilly the big beef bayonet the ladies favourite has slipped in nice and hard…"
I screamed at the top of my voice. The players' were all screaming and shouting because they'd won and one said: "Hey buddy, I ain't got a clue what you just said, but here is $25 to keep it up!"

"That's exactly what she said told me last night," I shot back to more roars of laughter. Dice never changes where ever you are in the world. Not that this particular boxman was impressed, "Don't you ever use that language on my table again!" he screamed with steam coming out of his ears. Lawrence looked at me to say, "Who's this wanker." Usually most of the tossers around the dice table are the ones tossing the dice. Talk about killing a game stone cold dead. The crew got the hump, and so did the players. This boxman was not playing cricket at all. There is always one.

Anyway, Mexico was a real trip because we docked at a place called Ensenada on the Baja Coast. The place was a real shithole, there was a great big stinking tuna factory in the actual port and the whole place reeked of rotting fish. The Mexican navy had their 'latest' warships moored here too; well they were probably the latest models during the First World War. I could not make my mind up, which was rotting the most, the fish, or the navy. The brilliant thing about working on this particular run was that you could sign off the ship in Ensenada on your day off, stay in a hotel overnight, and then get the public bus back up to San Diego. I did this once and once only. I cannot remember the name of the hotel I stayed in, but it was a highly regarded one in Ensenada and it was only $35 bucks a night. I watched the Star sail out of the harbour from my balcony and decided to do what any young man would do; I went on the fucking lash. I must admit the place had some wacky bars, I was standing outside one when two big fat American women came plunging down a fireman's pole. I asked the geezer on the door what the hell was going on here and he replied in broken English, "Se Señor, the only de a way out of de place is down the pole, Se. "Bloody hell, I'll have a bit of that and went up to see what shenanigans I could get myself into.

The place was crowded with a mixture of sailors, slappers and a sprinkling of tourists. Just my sort of joint. I managed to find a convenient place at the bar and there was already tequila awaiting me, served by a gorgeous Mexican girl with a huge pair of bumpers. As I tilted my head back, to down the drink, I nearly fell off my seat. On the wall behind the bar were loads of paintings, presumably done by the local artists. One of the pictures consisted of a males head, with a huge thick moustache and two sets of eyes. It did not matter how many times you looked at the picture, your own eyes just could not focus on it. I had never seen a picture quite like it; it was freaky yet brilliant at the same time. The Mexican girl whom had served me the drink started laughing; she informed me that everybody acts the same way when they first look at the picture. This bar was cool man, a mixture of the weird and the wonderful; I had never been in an establishment quite like it. The only thing I did not find appealing about being in Mexico was the food. I was about to order some from behind the bar, the girl insisted that this was one of the best eateries in town. Wherever I go in this world, I do three things first: I try the local beer to find out if it is good, I try the local cuisine, to get a flavour of the surroundings, and lastly, I try it on with the local women to see how much I can get away with. I will never forget my first week in Miami, I was in rolling around with an American girl, and she screamed out, "Yee Aahhh, take me round the back and ride me like a pony!" I fell off the fucking bed I was laughing so much. I was eyeing up the senorita behind the bar and, began to wonder if I would have such luck tonight.

"What are you grinning at señor," she asked with a smile on her face. "Nothing, nothing at all, just day dreaming…" I replied. I asked her what the local 'fish' was like; she smiled and informed me that it was very good last night. She also asked me how long I was planning to stay in Mexico for, and where I was staying. I told her that it was my first time here, and that I was staying in a hotel down-town. We had a good conversation for the next hour or so and, I was beginning to get wankered on the free tequila she kept offering. Some of the tourist girls wanted to dance with me, but my sights were firmly fixed on the beauty in front of me. I had never been to Mexico before - if you know what I mean. The flirtations had obviously gone up a notch or two and we eventually ended up whispering sweet nothings in each other's ears, I just could not wait to get this beauty back to the hotel. Then abruptly my world came crashing down. Some great big fat woman, with short hair and tattoos came out of the back room and started kissing my Mexican princess. I was gob smacked, she was a fucking carpet muncher, I could not believe it. "Hi," said the fat girl whilst grabbing a handful of that firm ass. My Mexican beauty smiled at me and said, "This is my partner Josie; Josie this is Windmill, he's from England".

"Hi Windmill, Windmill? You sure you ain't from Amsterdam?" said fat -so, whilst letting out the most dreadful laugh. Now I knew exactly what she meant when she said the 'fish' was good last night.

The trip down the fireman's pole was over in a flash and landed on my arse. It was a good gimmick for the bar, because there was another moron asking the same question I had asked several hours earlier. Ensenada was well dodgy after dark, the place was a shithole, and beggars were everywhere. I decided the best course of action to take after the disappointment in the bar, would be to head back towards the hotel. At least there, I could get even more wankered and would not have far to go when I passed out. In addition, I still had a chance to steam into the receptionist on duty.

Unfortunately, it was not going to be my night in Mexico because the receptionist happened to be a big hairy geezer and the lobby and the bar were virtually deserted. The following morning I got up early and went for breakfast, I initially tried the local concoction, but opted for the American styled offering because I had a three-hour bus journey back to the States, I did not want to spend half that time on the crapper. Even though I'd had lots of tequilas and no senoritas on this particular visit, I thought the experience was well worth it, well that was until I got the bus back. The fare to San Diego was peanuts; it was something like $10 one way.

Some geezer was hanging out the drivers cab shouting, "All aboard to the border, all aboard." I went up to him and inquired if this death trap was the bus for San Diego and, I asked him what our chances of actually making it were. "Se Señor Se, bus good bus, Se," he replied. I was far from convinced, but I had no choice but to hop aboard. Once onboard, things became surreal, the seats were actually wooden benches and the cabin was full of goats, chickens, and peasants. 'Oh fuck,' I thought, this is going to be interesting. I managed to claim a seat next to a big fat man whom was sweating like the proverbial pig he was. "Hey gringo, you wanna buy mescaline man?" said a young man sitting directly opposite me. No chance I thought to myself, this bus was already a trip; "No señor, no, thank you." The geezer leaned over, closer to me and asked, "What about a nice piece, err? My sister is sitting at the back man."

"Mate, fuck off!" I replied. I think he got the hint and he said something to his companion in Spanish, they both started laughing. Ten minutes later chitty, chitty- bang, bang was on the move; but a priest on a donkey overtook us. Gradually we made our way out of the city and the lingering stink of rotting fish soon evaporated with the beggars and the shanty houses. The road followed the Pacific Ocean and the bus seemed to be precariously hanging onto the cliff face, which we were ascending. Suddenly we were more than 150 feet above sea level and the poor old bus was clinging on for dear life. I dared not look out the window; there was only a matter of a few feet between us and a 150-foot drop into the deep blue sea and the lunatic, who was driving the thing, was all over the place. People were screaming and shouting, chickens were flying around the passageway, and smoke was coming from the engine compartment. 'Fucking hell' I thought to myself, if I am going to die, I might as well be off my rocker. I turned to my friend opposite and said, "I've changed my mind, gimme the mescaline man!"
The geezer handed me a small cactus, which was called peyote. "What the hell am I supposed to do with this?" I asked, somewhat bemused.

"Chew it man, chew it," replied the Mexican.

Twenty minutes later I was hanging out the fucking window and it was a real trip man. Suddenly the bus had taken on a completely new dimension. Everything seemed to going in slow motion, apart from 'speedy Gonzalez' whom was driving the bus. That lunatic appeared to be sitting on the actual steering wheel with his legs dangling out of the window. He turned to look at me and I fell off the buses bench; he had that same face has that picture in the bar, four eyes, and a big fuck off moustache.

I opened my eyes and the nutter was standing right over me, he was saying something, well his mouth was moving, but I could not hear any coherent words. "Arrhgggghhhh," I screamed and quickly closed my eyes again. Once my eyes had closed, another world opened. The whole bus was shaking from side to side, like the ship coming out of the harbour in San Diego, so I opened my eyes again and, for some reason crawled to the back of the bus, under the seats. Everybody had huge feet, one geezer had webbed toes; this was getting to be too fucking freaky. Something was tugging at my leg; I looked around to see this ten-foot chicken trying to drag me back up the bus. I closed my eyes for a split second and when I opened them, I was driving the bus. "Ooh shit," I screamed, because the steering wheel did not work properly, every time I turned the wheel left, the bus went right, and vice versa. Suddenly everybody was screaming because a chicken had managed to get between the windshield and me. The thing was flying at eye level and there

were feathers everywhere. I could not see a thing, I tried
to bat it out of the way, but the steering wheel came off in
my hand. The wind caught it and it flew out of the
window, now we had no steering wheel. All the Mexicans
were shouting in Spanish and I began to laugh
hysterically, it was wild man. I was not looking at the
road anymore, I was facing the passengers on the bus,
laughing at them, and they all looked like cacti. They
were all pointing and shouting for me to look ahead and
when I did, the bus had plunged off the cliff and was
nose-diving towards the sea. Even I began screaming, it
was like a choir from hell: "Arrrgghhhhhh."
We seemed to be falling forever, there was an old ship on
the ocean, and we were heading straight for it. I was
shouting at them to get out of the fucking way; a geezer
looked up from the deck, it was Odysseus.

"Señor, señor, is you OK?" said the Mexican fella
whom had supplied me the peyote. I must have been
dreaming: 'Eh? Where am I? Are we in the underworld?'
I said dazed and confused. It took several seconds for my
eyes to focus. I was still on the bus, and we were still 200
feet up a mountain cliff whilst the sea sparkled below. I
went to the bathroom and my eyes were like saucepans,
pupils the size of footballs. "Oh shit," I said to myself,
and started laughing again. There was a knock at the door,
"Hey señor, you want some more mescaline's," asked the
Mexican. I declined his offer, anymore of that crap and I
would be in a wormhole, transporting myself around the

universe in Mr. Hawking's wheelchair. The final hour or so of the journey I sat in solitude, I could not look, or engage in any form of conversation with anybody. If I did, I would have immediately burst out into fits of laughter. My face was stuck to the window like glue, under the effects of the hallucinogenic, it was. Back in San Diego I made my way to the Star, I bumped into some of the lads on the gangway, they asked about my little adventure in Ensenada. "It was a real trip," I said smiling. The lads just looked at each other and laughed, I am sure they had done exactly the same things on numerous occasions themselves.

One of the girls in the casino who was a cashier, was onboard the Greek ship Oceanos, which sank off South Africa. She was telling us how the Greek officers and Captain had abandoned the ship, and left all the passengers and crew to their own devices. I briefly remembered seeing it on CNN a year previously, and I remembered a girl being winched off the funnel as the ship was in her death throes. That girl was sitting right in front of us now. She showed us a cut out from the British newspaper the Daily Mail, and the interview she had given during her harrowing experience. I was amazed, I asked her how did she find the courage to go back on a ship, and did she really trust the crews anymore.
"It was not the crew whom had let anybody down; they were the real hero's that day," she replied. But she resented all Greek officers now, because they swanked

around the ship, giving orders like they were the Gestapo, but when the shit it the fan, they were cowards and ran. "Captain fucking calamity decided the best course of action to take was to leave the passengers to their own devices. He simply packed his stuff, and decided the best way to conduct the evacuation of the vessel was actually from the shore," she said. We were all stunned. I felt for her, we all did, what a remarkable woman. I asked for a short contract on the ship, I was knackered and needed a break. The company was great and said I could go, but it could only be for a few months. This suited me because I could recharge my batteries, so I was to be back in England for the summer. I did not yet know it, but the next placement on a ship was going to have profound implications for the next ten years. On the way back to the UK on an American Airlines flight some sexy black hostess was all over me like a rash. That was a bloody first!

GUAM ISLAND

A rep from Tiber called a few months later and wanted to know if I was interested in going to Guam. "Guam, where the hell is that," I asked.
"It's in the middle of the Pacific. You'll be working on a daily ship called The Tropic Star if you fancy it."
"Yeah, fuck it...why not, sounds like something different," I replied. A week later I was booked on the flight from hell, I could not believe it when the itinerary

came in the post, I had to fly from Birmingham to London; London to LA; LA to Hawaii and then Hawaii to Guam. From my front door in England to the gangway of the Tropic Star took over 34 hours. I eventually arrived and made my way to the purser's office to sign on, 'Stormin Spalding' came down to the crew office to say hello and he showed me around the casino and the ship. Stevie Hayward was also onboard, he was the geezer whom gave us the table test for Tiber back in Miami.

None of the other casino employees' had arrived yet, many were still in transit from their homes or other ships. Therefore, I went to the cabin and had a 'power nap.' The next day most of the casino crew turned up, my cabin mate was a geezer from Southampton in England, his name was Dave, and he seemed pretty laid back and cool. I went to the back deck with Spalding and he introduced me to the others, including a young woman from Nassau Bahamas. During the first few days in Guam, all the crew spent time within the casino going over the various procedures they expected us to follow. Most of the casino crew were cool, but again it was a completely different crowd to the Atlantic lot. The situation with the women on board was not too good. Most of the girls had embarked has couples and the rest seemed to be a mixture of slappers and old boilers.

The first cruise was unbelievably cushy, our schedule was the easiest I had ever known on any ship. The boat sailed out of the harbour at 5-30pm, the casino was only allowed to open between 6 & 10pm, and then were back alongside the dock at 10-30pm. Have a bit of that! Guam was a strange island, the locals- the Chamorro's, were the weirdest bunch of people you would ever come across. Nobody could quite figure them out, they were really fucking out there man. Guam has a huge American naval base and apparently it had 'kicked off' big time with the Japanese during WWII. One of the bars everybody used to hang in called, 'The Jungle,' was full of sailors and slappers. One night I was dancing around with the Bahamian bird from Nassau, well I was trying to dance, I needed some lessons in the art of winding. After that night, we became good friends and she was forever around my cabin. Some of the others seemed to be quite content to fuck off to The Jungle every night and talk shit about work. We had other ideas, firstly we found a club called the Underground. This place was a dance sort of club full of carpet munchers and sausage jockeys. Nevertheless, the club played the only progressive music on the island. Most of the people were cool, even if they were all benders. We made friends with a pair of faggots called Dan and Mario, one was the son of a wealthy Australian real estate tycoon and the other was a local. Guam really was the easy life as far as we were concerned because the work was so fucking easy. If the ship sailed with one hundred guests it was busy, and only thirty of those would turn up in the casino. You may be forgiven

for thinking, 'yeah it's all nice and dandy working 20hrs a week, but the pay must have been shit.' Truth is, the few players who came into the casino regularly were rich Koreans and we averaged $500/600 + a week.
I can guarantee you no dealers, on any ship anywhere in the world worked a measly 20hrs and received a minium of 500 bucks. Therefore, we had plenty of time off for our drinking contests.

Brendon, one of the older dealers on the ship was a riot, he used to sit in the middle of his cabin reading his newspaper all night long. The only problem with this was his cabin mate could never get into his cabin. All the dealers would steam into his cabin for a few sherbets after work, and to listen to his bollocks. Brendon would always give us all a lecture about the "good old days," once he'd had a skinful. "You fucking kids don't know anything about the casinos, or what we used to get up to," he would say, slurring his words. "You whipper snappers...blah blah blah," you get the fucking drift. Eventually Brendon would fall asleep – usually with a bottle in his hand, whilst snoring like a trooper. Once this happened, we'd all fuck off because of the noise, or simply sit outside his cabin in the corridor. One night some of the boys managed to get some make-up off one of the girls and proceeded to 'paint him up' whilst in his drunken stupor. Several hours later, Brendon somehow awoke more pissed than when he went to sleep and came out of the cabin into the corridor calling us all "poofs" and

"faggots." The beer he'd fallen asleep with was still in his hand, but he hadn't noticed the pink nail varnish on his fingers, or the red lipstick on his lips. From that day forward he was affectionately known as Brenda the Benda. Brenda started his usually rant,"You fucking kids...you now nothing about..."
"Drag?" interrupted one of the boys.
Brendon looked on, confused.

The only real concern about living in this part of the world were the typhoons. Guam was located right in the middle of typhoon alley, and whilst the ship was there, we got hit five times. Super Typhoon Omar was by far the worst and it caused utter devastation to Guam. Furthermore, it nearly sank the fucking ship!
With this monster storm fast approaching Guam, we were unexplainably still tied up at the dock after the previous nights cruise. What usually happens when a storm is approaching, the ship 'runs' from it - or in layman's terms, simply fucks off as fast as it can to minimize damage. So for the crew to awake and find ourselves still at the dock mystified us all. Eventually Capt. Chaos decided to leave the harbour, and once outside the breakwater, we all knew we were in for a rough ride.

The weather was already very nasty, the wind speed had picked up dramatically and the swell in the ocean was fearsome. I could sense certain uneasiness amongst the ship's crew, everyone had a look of deep concern written across their faces. For several hours the wind and the waves steadily grew, it soon became clear that we were deep in the shit. Some of us decided to go down to the rope deck and see how bad the situation really was.

Ten minutes later the Bahamian turned up too, we were standing there for about twenty minutes and the waves were getting bigger and bigger. "Fuck, look at that," said one of the boys as a huge wave slam into the side of the ship. The ship listed heavily to starboard. "Woo," we all shouted in unison. The ship righted herself only to be met by another huge wave and it slammed hard against the hull, this time we were all knocked off our feet.

"Fuck," shouted the Bahamian. All of us felt very uneasy about that last wave, and as the ship tried to right herself we were greeted with a horrifying sight. A huge wall of water, at least thirty - feet high, was rushing towards us. We were at least twenty feet from the ocean on the rope deck and all you could see was this towering colossus bearing down on us. We all screamed and ran towards the entrance that led into the vessel. The wave hit the ship like a bomb, water rushed onto the rope deck like a torrent and would certainly have washed us over the side. The passageway I was standing in contained fire extinguishers and other pieces of equipment, it had all been dislodged; the ship was that far over I was virtually standing on the walls. One of the extinguishers had ruptured, a thick white powder was spraying itself into the corridors, and you could hear screaming from within the ship, things were getting broken and people were panicking. On the back deck I was praying, this time I did not believe the ship had any chance of righting herself, she was hard over.

Looking out into the ocean for that split second, I could see the menace and anger of the ocean, it was frighteningly beautiful, almost like a war had broken out and we were in no man's land. Come on, come on! I kept thinking to myself, it seemed like the ship was over for an eternity; things were flashing through my mind, everybody had ran into the ship. I was calling them because I really felt that we would all soon be in the water, that the ship would be lost and they had little chance within the vessel. The ship had a deathly silence; I could no longer hear the engines, only the screams of the wind and the ferocious hammering of the waves. The water was like a frothing volcano, brilliant shades of blue mixed with white foaming spray and amongst it all, the colours of the rainbow. What seemed like an eternity lasted literally less than a minute, the ship groaned and slowly, very slowly, she balanced herself once again. I thanked the Gods', Poseidon in particular. When things go wrong at sea they happen quickly, very quickly, my heart was racing and I immediately went inside the ship to see the carnage. Everything was upon its side, dislodged and piled up on the starboard side of the vessel. Items within the gift shops were smashed to pieces; in the casino, some of the tables had tipped over, in the restaurant tables, chairs and cutlery were strewn everywhere. The crew had an hesitant look about them now, we had all felt the danger and you could sense the uneasiness amongst us all. Word soon spread that the ship had actually been two degree's away from capsize. The bridge had lost control of the engines for several minutes and if the ship had taken another wave on the broadside, it would have been all over. Some of the girls were crying others were hiding in their cabins. I went up to the bridge to find out what was going on, because the weather was getting worse by the hour.

The captain along with the chief engineer looked concerned; they hardly spoke a word, yet gazed out of the bridge windows in awe. "In twenty five years at sea, I have never seen such a restless ocean," said the captain. Who he was talking to, I cannot say. I think he was talking to himself, he too looked in shock. The bow of the ship was pounding into the huge waves that came relentlessly and these waves must have been at least thirty feet in height. The sky was angry; the clouds above had taken on a sinister shape and colour, everything looked menacing. We tried desperately to find safe shelter in the outer harbour of Yap Island. The ship had found brief sanctuary on the lee side of the winds, but it was a precariously dangerous situation. The ship required constant movement to battle the swells. Twenty-four hours later, we were making our way back to Guam, the anger of the sea was subsiding slightly, and we were informed that the typhoon was moving away.

Rumours started to circulate amongst the crew that the port authorities had given the Capt. of the Star the wrong information regarding the storm, that they instructed him to sail north instead of south, and virtually right into the typhoon. This caused a lot of anger amongst the crew. Surely, the captain had the necessary equipment onboard to view the formation of weather patterns. Why did he stay in the harbour that night in Guam? Was it his incompetence or was it the fault of the coast guard in Guam? Many conspiracy theories circulated amongst us, one being that the Chamorro's had intentionally given the captain the wrong information because the religious organizations on the island where strenuously against gambling. They did not want the ship in the harbour to tempt their flocks to the sinful pastime of gambling. In fact there had been several articles written in the local newspaper which venomously opposed the Tropic Star, and the paper actually called for a national boycott.

We returned to the harbour to find utter devastation, the island had taken a direct hit. The trees had been stripped of their leaves, many more, totally flattened. The wind had been that ferocious over the island that it had ripped the tarmac off the car park, nobody had ever seen anything like it. War ships in the naval dock, wrenched from their moorings, and washed up on the beach like coconuts. The road towards town had virtually washed away; a bomb from WWII washed by the Seaman's Centre. Smashed boats lay silent witness on the beach, paying testament to the devastatingly powerful fury of Mother Nature. We did not work for the next five days, nobody could get to the ship, the roads needed urgent repairs, but the local authorities had matters that were more pressing. Some of us walked the few miles down to the town and it was a shambles. No electricity, no telephones and no water, everything was in chaos, it was like a war zone. Eventually over the next few weeks things were slowly getting back to some sort of normality, the ship was back in business, but the rumours floating around were that the ship would not stay here for too much longer. It was not economically viable.

Storming Spalding informed the Bahamian and me that we would be signing off the ship within the next few weeks. Our contracts were up. He also said that we were both booked on the same flight to Hawaii, we had an overnight in LA, then we would both be flying on to Miami, where we had another overnight. From there we parted company, because Judy was booked on a flight to Nassau and I was booked on a flight to London. We had had a good time in Guam together and now the party was almost over, both of us seemed to be quiet about the whole episode, we really did not say that much initially. "What you going to do on your vacation Windmill," she asked. "I dunno, maybe chill out for a few days, then go to Amsterdam," I said. We had become good mates, and we both agreed it might be a good idea to continue the party in Europe. Tiber was in all essence a good company

to work for because not only did we miss a week's work because of the typhoon, we also missed the majority of our wages, tips. Spalding arranged a big party for all of us, and the company gave each dealer something like $1600 a head for all the stress and missed pay.
They certainly did not have to do this, and the whole casino was very appreciative of this gesture of good will.

We eventually arrived in LA and made our way to the hotel, which was located just off the world famous Sunset Blvd. That evening we went to the legendary 'Whiskey a Go, Go' Club and a few other fine bars along the strip. The next day we were in Miami and we stayed right on Biscayne Blvd, I went over the bridge to the port and got a ticket to Nassau. The next morning we arrived at Paradise Island Airport, and on the way to her house house I remembered that strange feeling I'd had on the back deck of the Majestic a couple of years previously. However, the next day I had some bad news from England, my brother had been sent to prison for a few years, and since my family had been expecting me to return, I had to go back. The Bahamian wasn't really upset, a bit sad perhaps and I was too in reality, but I really had to go. We promised each other that we would stay in touch, that afternoon I went to get a ticket to London, and by 5pm, I was gone.

GAME CHANGER

Back in England, it was a double whammy, my brother had been sent down for some dodgy crime they had accused him of committing, and the plans I had discussed with the Bahamian bird had seemed to disintegrate within 24hrs. It was early march and it was freezing cold. Guam was such a hot and humid place that my body could not adjust to the British weather, I spent the first two days in my bed. I would not come out of it; it was that fucking cold. The Bahamian, or jungle woman as I liked to call her, called from the Bahamas and asked me what I was doing. I told her I was sitting by the fire and she thought the fucking house was on fire. The phone calls between us became more frequent and then one night she called and said, "I will be in England in 10 days. I'm flying into Manchester; will you come and pick me up?"

Me and my old mate Bob the nob went up to Manchester to get her, she was standing outside the airport in a huge trench coat, shivering. I walked up behind her and tapped her on the back, "Aargh" she screamed, we hugged, and it was good to see her again. "Its fucking freezing man!" We had a wild time in England. We went to London and Amsterdam that Easter, but we would virtually run out of money after a few months. A rep from the office in Miami called and asked me if I was ready to come back yet. I told the Bahamian girl from Guam was here in England too, and could they put us on the same ship if possible. "Yeah, no problem. Leave it with me and I'll sort you both something out within the next week or so." Two weeks later we flew back into Miami and signed on the *SS Norway*. The Norway was a monster of a ship; it was fucking huge. The Norway was originally the SS France, one of the true great transatlantic super-liners left. Unfortunately, they had added a few decks to her, which altered her striking lines somewhat; however, at least she'd been saved from the scrap yard. She wasn't sailing the Atlantic anymore either, she was now based in Miami sailing the Caribbean.

Strangely enough, I never had the pleasure of working with Nobby for AA, our paths had never crossed in the company, yet here we were, working in the same casino again since those initial days at Cromwell's back in Birmingham. We had only been on the ship for less than a month when jungle woman said she was ill and was going to see the doctor. Things were going to change considerably; she returned looking like she had seen a ghost. "What's up? You OK, what did the doc says?" I asked her. She said nothing and sat down; I again asked what the problem was. "Windmill, I'm pregnant," she said after several minutes. I was dumbfounded, I seemed to lose all composure, and my jaw dropped open. I think both of us were in shock, neither of us said a word for what seemed like an eternity. "What are we to do?" she said; I was still in shock, but eventually replied, "Well this changes everything, I mean, who's the dad? Wow, I thought you said that you couldn't get…" I was interrupted, "I know, that's what the doctor said in Nassau, I'm shocked too, what are we going to do Windmill, and what do you mean who's the fucking dad?" She immediately went rushing around the ship informing all the girls in the casino. I had thoughts of jumping over the side and making a swim for it. London calling by the Clash kept ringing in my head. That night in the casino on the dice table I was getting a right ribbing from the boys, they loved it. "Fucking Windmill's gonna be a father? Fuckin god help us all, the thought of another like him running riot around the world doesn't bear thinking about." There was a problem with the Norway though, it was the toughest ship in the fleet to work on because it had three sea days and JW – jungle woman, was getting tired. So I went to see the boss, Tommy Lardy, and asked him if we could be transferred to a ship that visited Nassau more frequently. I said this would be beneficial for several reasons: namely, it was close to home for JW, so that she could go regularly to see her doctor, and that when the time comes for her to disembark the company would save money from air tickets and hotels. He immediately said "No," and walked off. I thought his attitude was rather strange to say the least, some of the boys said he did not like his best staff asking to leave. It was not about leaving, it was about necessity, and from that day forward, I thought the guy was odd. The situation was going to get even worse; JW went into the office in

Miami on the next port day and spoke with the boss. A few days into the new cruise, I was pulled off the dice table and told to go into the office. Tommy was in there and he coldly said, "Why are you always laughing and joking around with everybody? Are you taking drugs? I want you to go down to the hospital immediately for a drugs test." I was flabbergasted, and then all hell broke loose. "You've got to be fucking joking Tommy, what's this really about? Is it…"

"Don't you fucking swear at me," he raged. "Bollocks, just because we asked for a transfer, you're trying to get me fired, is that it?" I raged back, "You're suspended, get downstairs to your cabin immediately until further notice," he screamed. "Fuck off," I yelled back, then things became even more heated because we nearly started fighting in his office; one of the pit bosses had to drag me out. I went straight down to the crew bar; I was shaking with the adrenalin and needed a beer. JW came rushing down looking distraught, "What's going on?" she screamed. I told her and she was in shock. I really thought he was going to sign me off the ship in St Thomas the following morning, and I would be going home that day. Fuck me, how situations can change so quickly. Several hours later, I got a call from one of the pit bosses in my cabin, "Windmill can you please come up to Tommy's office now." I went up, expecting to be told the bad news. I entered the office and Tommy was standing there with Ron, "Why did JW and you go behind my back and ask for a transfer?" he asked coldly in his Welsh accent. "Tommy, nobody went behind anybodies back! We asked you for a transfer and you said no. That was that as far as we were concerned; JW bumped into the boss on her way to the store, and she was asking her about the Norway, JW said she liked the ship, but because she was now pregnant she was finding it hard. The boss asked her if she wanted a transfer, with me, to a ship that went to Nassau, because it would not be a problem. That's all that happened Tommy I swear." I said to him. "Well you are going to be signing off in St Thomas on Tuesday morning; both of you, you're transferring to *The Westward* which sails out of Fort Lauderdale." Then he just turned his back, I did not say another word, and left the office. We said our goodbye's to all the casino crew and suddenly we were in Lauderdale.

Even to this day, I hold no animosity towards the fella; I just thought his method of dealing with situations was bizarre. We signed of in St Thomas and flew to San Juan, from there straight to Fort Lauderdale to join the MS Westward. The Westward turned out to be one of the best ships in the fleet to work on, it was only a three and four day cruise ship, and it had two overnights in Nassau. Stevie Hayward was the manager so we knew things were going to be easy. We were making good money too, almost $1000 every week. The cabins were huge, they'd cut the ship in half when she was known as the Royal Viking Star, and put another 100 feet in the middle, fuck knows how they did it, but it was done. The casino staff had all the new cabins and the crew bar was brilliant and led onto the back deck.

The funniest thing happened on the Westward, some geezer had come on, and he just could not lose playing blackjack. Nobody could figure out what he was up to, he just kept on winning. The manager asked me if I thought he was card counting, I told him I had never seen a card counter that good. The dealer would be showing a six, and he would take a card on 16, and pull a 5. As if he knew, what cards were coming next; as it turned out, he did. The office's security came on the next cruise and examined the cards. They were actually marked, but you could only see the cards with a pair of tinted glasses. It just so happens that the guy was wearing such a pair. The next question was how did he get the cards? Well we never locked the cards in the safe after the casino closed. We just sorted them out and locked them in the podium in the pit. They wanted to know how did he get into the podium, because there was no sign of forced entry; had somebody in the casino actually given him a key, or a copy of that key? The next thing to happen was probably one of the most bizarre episodes I'd ever encounter upon a ship. All the casino staff had to take a lie detector test in Lauderdale; it was freaky man. They plastered us in wires and asked us questions like these:

"Did ya mark the cards; and is the man related to you?"

"Have you ever stolen from the casino before?"

"When are you going to get your cut of the money?"

"Have you tried the same scam in Vegas?"

It was scary, because they just bombarded you with questions like this. Nobody was charged or suspected of any wrongdoing and, the whole thing to this day remains a mystery to this very day. Nobody in the casino failed the test, so they assumed the geezer must have done it all by himself. Possibly coming into the casino one night and waiting for it to close to see where the cards were stashed. Because in those days there was no CCTV in the casinos on any ships, he could simply turn up in the middle of the night and open the podium with a simple screwdriver, mark the cards and put them back again.

The Westward was easy work, and we visited Nassau on Tuesdays and Saturdays for overnights. Most of the casino employees hated Nassau, and to be honest most of the crews of any ship hate Nassau, because it is expensive, and the people can be rather arrogant and rude. I'm not saying this to be negative about Nassau, it was just the opinion people had whilst on the ships. Stevie, our manager had served his contract and he was replaced by a woman called Sally Dearly. She was your typical English bird: peroxide spiky hair, huge tits and plastered in make-up. I liked her though, she was value for money, and she was always shit-faced at the bar and left the casino to run itself. One Sunday morning we were all over at the legendary Drop Off Bar in Nassau and it was time to head back to the ship. We sailed at 6am and it was nearly 5.30am now. Everybody was back apart from Dealy, whom was in a punch up with another boiler over a fella. By 5.55am, they started the engines and the rope guys were preparing to cast off. At 5.59 all ropes were let loose and the thrusters kicked in, the ship began to slowly leave the dock; at 6.00am exactly, Dealy came running down the fucking dock in her stilettos, hands holding up her skirt, shouting at the top of her voice, "Wait for fucking me you bastard's!" Later that day the security guard was crying with laughter has he told us what actually happened. On his radio, he informed the bridge: "Casino manager running down dock! Casino manager jumping for the ship! Casino manager in the water." everybody was howling with laughter, they had to fish her out of the sea. Apparently, she looked like a wet trout when they finally pulled her onboard.

JW gave birth in mid December. Things back on the ship were going to change drastically too though. The Westward was going to be sold off to another cruise company, and everybody had to take vacation or transfer to a ship of the company's choice. I had already done seven months on her, so it was obvious that I would be sent on vacation. 'Oh well, nice knowing ya Ms. Bahamas, I hope the kid doesn't turn out like me,' this is just one of the letters I had written out, intending to leave the fucker outside her front door as I prepared to piss off to the Airport! Unfortunately, I must have been going soft in my old age, morality got the better of me, and I decided to stay. It was going to be tough though because it was impossible at this time for an ex-pat to work in either of the casinos in Nassau; the government would not allow such things. JW who had once worked on Paradise Island, said in all probability, it would take several months to regain her job back there. I had exactly six weeks to try to save enough money for us to be reasonably comfortable for a few months, but we needed to think hard about the future. I told JW to submit all the necessary paper work to Paradise Island and that we would return to England whilst things were sorted out, at least in the UK I could earn some money in a casino. I signed off the Westward in March and flew straight to Nassau, the company had already brought me a ticket to Britain and I got them both return tickets at a discount rate from the office in Miami. Therefore, by April, the three of us were living at my parent's house, they both had two-month open tickets, so if anything went wrong for any reason, they could fly back to the Bahamas.

Whilst at home the phone rang and I was offered a position on a world cruise ship called The Crown Odyssey, which was presently in Europe and sailing out of Tilbury, London. It was going from England to: Germany, Finland, Denmark, Sweden, Norway, and Russia, with an overnight in Copenhagen and three overnights in St Petersburg Russia. This was the first cruise and then it was doing the land of the midnight sun, where the ship made its way up and down the Norwegian fjords, and then into the Arctic Circle. Because we were basically hard up for cash without any income, I decided to go. JW too was offered a position; however, because of the situation with the nipper it was impossible. My parents said they had no problem watching the youngster whilst JW got the chance to see Northern Europe and Russia. A few days later, my brother gave a ride down to Tilbury to join the ship. "Don't fuck about on the ship mate," he said. "Who me? Nah mate, you must have surely got me mixed up with somebody else," I replied. I signed on, went to my cabin then went wandering around the ship to see what it was like. I must say it was extremely posh. That evening the ship pulled away from her berth and made her way down the River Thames. I donned my tuxedo and made my way up to the casino to see what sort of action we were going to get on here. Needless to say, the casino was very quiet, and the casinos staff were all chilled souls and extremely friendly. You can tell within seconds on a ship what sorts of clientele are onboard ships as soon as the casino opens. On gambling ships, they come charging in dressed in t-shirts and flip-flops. On mediocre cruise ships, it is usually a mixture of jeans and polo shirts. This ship happened to be on a whole new level. It was in a different class to anything I had worked on previously, the vessel was full of extremely wealthy individuals, dripping in money.   For the very first and last time on a ship, I never saw any male guest wearing anything less than a suit, or the female guests wearing dresses. The people onboard were obviously extremely wealthy. They had to be, the cheapest fourteen-night cruise was something like $12-500. The casino crew were allowed to eat with the passengers in the main dining room, providing you wore your tuxedo, or the girls full evening dress, and the food was scrumptious. Filet Mignon and Lobster with peach and tomato soup was heaven. Even in the crew mess, sirloin steak and chips were on the menu every single night.

The ports were also superb and the highlight of the cruise was, for many people, especially the American guests on board, Russia. It was 1994 and the country was still shaking off the shackles of its communist past. The City of St Petersburg was caught in a time warp, the decadence of the place was astounding, and in its heyday, it would have been the jewel in the crown for Russians. Obviously inspired by the renaissance of Europe, the public buildings were breathtakingly beautiful. The winter palace of Peter the Great confirmed this with its opulent demeanour. The palace is indeed now home to probably the finest museum in the world, the Hermitage. The exhibits are unequalled by any museum upon this Earth. Those two weeks flew by and before I knew it, we were back in London. JW came down to Tilbury with my brother during our next turn around, she was not happy.

She thought I was gallivanting around Europe whilst she was stuck at home with the kid. I informed her that she would be signing on the ship after the next cruise. I gave her all the money I had earnt from the previous one to shut her up. This pacified her briefly, and she went back slightly happier. Anyway, I have again cut out some of the juicer parts what happened on this fucking ship, but will tell you the jungle woman signed on for 14 days, and we both resigned after getting into a fight with an officer.

Back in sunny Birmingham JW had a call from Nassau saying that all her paper work was in order and she was due to return to work at Paradise Island. I did not leave with her because there was no point at this time because I was unable to work there. Therefore, I managed to find employment in a casino in Birmingham until things got easier in Nassau. The same GM from my first club Cromwell's' now ran Sergeant Yorke's on the corner of Gas and Broad St in Birmingham. The job did not last that too long though, the Bahamian kept saying that she needed help in Nassau with the kid, so within a month or so I was back on the island with the island girl. However, this time I had moved into her mom's house. I was not sure at all if I was doing the right thing, what was happening to me? Had I gone completely nuts?
Her family was cool though and I really liked her step dad Johnny, he was a cool American fella of high intelligence, very reserved but intriguing when you could get him to talk. The only problem he had was that he was a

recovering alcoholic, his wife figured I would at some point lead him down the garden path, she was right.

JW was acting strange; she would suddenly become a slightly different person now she was back in her environment. I really did not take that much notice to be honest, but we did have quite a few arguments over nothing really. I certainly had not flown across to Nassau to sit at home with the kid all day whilst she was in the casino. No way, fuck that, so I headed off down to Nassau Harbour and managed to get a job on a ship called The Atlantic. These days you cannot do such things because of security checks everywhere after 9/11. However, back in the day, you could literally walk up any ships gangway in port, and ask one of the officers to call the casino manager. The MV Atlantic was an older ship, in fact she was the sister ship of the Majestic, and was in Nassau twice a week. Nigel Neilson was the manager; he was an old Tiber Trading boy and a cracking lad. His missus Sandra was on board too and she was a real nutter, but good fun. My cabin mate was a slot tech called Charlie from Scotland and he was cool too, everything on the ship was good. Another geezer from Scotland was a bloke called Jim. Bit of a nutter, but a good laugh. He was forever paranoid because he thought the company were about to fire his ass, so one day he had the bright idea of jumping ship and trying his luck in New York. They promoted me to pit boss within a month and I got my own cabin. The crew on here were superb, even the officers were dead cool; everybody was onboard for the good times.

Any casino lad will tell you it does not take long to be seduced by the affections of a bevy of beauties, and one lad certainly was no different in that respect. Indeed, he had five different girlfriends on the Atlantic, the sexiest being a Scottish stunner called Valerie; she had the looks and body of a model; long black curly hair and sparkling blue eyes. What a jammy bastard! If I hadn't have met the jungle woman this really could have been me! One night we were all having a few beers in a cabin when she came in drunk and sat on my mates knee. Anyway, she wanted to use the restroom, but somebody was already in there, so he said, "Here, use mine...oh and if you want to lie down just jump straight in and I'll be around in five." As she got up off his knee, he gave her a right old slap on the arse. She turned around and smiled.

"Fucking hell mate! You jammy bastard, I think you're in there," I said. Everybody on the ship had chased her, yet nobody had managed to slip her a crippler.

"Nah, she is out of my league mate. That bloke from the gift shop has been trying for weeks, flowers, chocolate, romantic dinners, hasn't he banged her yet?" he asked.

"Nah, she ain't freed it up for nobody," said another with a look of disappointment on his face. An hour later, we were all laughing and fucking around as per usual, and then I realized I was opening the casino at midday.

"Right lads, that's me. Make sure you're all up and ship shape and Bristol fashion in the morning." I went to my cabin, stripped off and jumped into my bunk. The bloke who had slapped Val's ass lived next door and because the walls within the cabins are wafer thin, I'm sure I could hear some fucker in there. I put a pint glass to the wall so I could hear better, "Fucking hell Val! You're naked!" I heard. The jammy bastard! For the next hour or so all I could hear was, thud, thud, thud and howling as our man pounded away for Queen and Country. Good lad!

I think he ended up seeing her for a while, I know she went to his cabin every night because I had my pint glass firmly planted to the cabin wall. He very discreet about the whole situation and nobody knew - well apart from me and everybody I had told. A few weeks later all the lads from the casino were in my cabin having a few beers after work, and some of the gift shop people came down too for a few scoops and a laugh.
"Where is Valerie?" asked Adrian, the guy who had invested a serious amount of time and money trying to prise open her legs.
"Fuck knows, probably getting her beauty sleep," said Nigel the manager.
"You look sad Adrian, what is up mate?" asked Jim, one of the casino boys.
"Nothing really mate, I think I'm in love," he replied grinning.
"What with our Val? I replied.

"Yes mate, me and her are on the threshold. I have nearly cracked it," he answered smiling.

"Cracked what?" Asked Jim. Adrian hushed his voice so nobody could hear him outside the cabin, leaned forward and said, "You lot ain't got a clue about women, sitting down here all night getting pissed. Birds ain't interested in that, they like a bit of class," he replied, whilst using his hands to brush his shoulders.

"Really?" Said Nigel.

"Yeah really; come on lads birds like that are high class, you can't take em down the crew bar and buy em a pint now can you? You have to wine and dine them in fine restaurants, buy them flowers and leave them little presents to let them know you are sincere. I know it probably all sounds a bit too romantic for you boozers, but a quality girl likes quality things. Why do you think she is in bed now? Because she wants to look radiant tomorrow for me," replied Adrian.

"Nope, she's been banging him for the last two weeks and needs a fucking rest!" answered Nigel whilst pointing at Jim. We were in hysterics. Poor old Adrian had a look of utter shock on his face. I have never seen anybody's blood drain so quickly out of somebody's face that quick before. After a few minutes, he said to Jim, "Is it true?" Jim was looking at the floor trying not to laugh, but he eventually looked him in the eye and replied, "Yes mate, I have been stuffing her like a spring chicken."

Everybody was howling with laughter, well everybody

128

apart from poor old Adrian, who got up and stormed out of the cabin in a strop! People who join ships looking for love, or think they're in love, learn some very harsh lessons incredibly quickly.

Back to business side of things, everything on the ship was plain sailing and the casino had a wicked sound system. Peavey bass bins and speakers all around the gaming floor. One day I was standing under this big black box stroking my chin, when Charlie walked up, he too looked up at the sub woofer and said, "Look nice in your apartment in Nassau when you sign off Windmill." "Yes indeed mate, yes indeed...I wonder...," I replied. Several hours later Charlie was doing his daily inspection of the gaming machines and just happened to have a small pair of ladders, a tape measure and a pencil behind his ear. Quick as a flash, he had measured the width, depth and height of the bass bin. Later that afternoon whilst down in our cabin he passed me the slip of paper upon which he had written down the exact measurements. Wide-eyed and bushy tailed I yelped, "Thanks!" and quickly scarped down to the carpentry shop within the depths of the vessel. I gave the geezer the note, asked him to knock up the box, cut to two 3-inch circles exactly 24inchs apart and paint it black. I gave him a crisp $20 bill for his troubles. Later that evening whilst the manager decided it was quiet enough for him to disappear for an hour or so, Charlie and me swung into action! I legged it down to the carpentry shop and collected the merchandise, then made a beeline straight for the casino floor. Charlie already had the ladders ready with the necessary tools to make the switch. Most of the dealers were howling with laughter, they just could not believe we had the cheek to knock off the speaker in full view of the customers or crew. It took literally seconds to swap the empty box for the prized sub woofer and unless you had an ear for sound, you could not tell the difference! What sort of idiot would hang a bass bin from the ceiling anyway? They are supposed to be on the floor! I dashed down the cabin and stashed the box, when we docked in Nassau in the morning, the box would take centre stage around Crabby St. Later that evening in the pit, I asked Nigel if I should crank up the sound system in the casino, he briefly looked around, looked directly at our home-made box and said, "Nah, it sounds just right to me." Grinning from ear to ear, I turned and winked at Charlie, who was shaking his head whilst running his hand over his face.

After delivering the box to Nassau, we returned to Canaveral. I had to meet a new sign on in the terminal and show him to the crew office, his cabin and around the ship. Colin Pleb was waiting patiently in the far corner of the terminal sweating like a pig. The geezer was a Brummie and had a wicked sense of humour too, he stank of booze and I immediately suspected this geezer was going to be a riot on the ship. Three days earlier, another new hire, an eastern European dealer called Liz, a sexy little number who could hardly speak any English turned up. Everybody in the casino presumed because she was new, and her English not the best she was a bit shy. Shy my arse! On her second cruise she turned up for her shift in the shortest miniskirts I had ever seen, you could literally see the cheeks of her ass has she walked around the casino pit. Pled was obviously a streetwise geezer and clocked it straight away, he definitely was not shy at all! "Oi Windmill, why don't you send Liz to do a bit of dice training when she returns from her break," asked Pled, who had just returned from a break and who had obviously received an eyeful of eastern promise.

"Good fucking thinking mate, we'll stick her straight on third base, she doesn't need to learn the stick just yet," I replied grinning from ear to ear. Ten minutes later Liz returned from her coffee break. "Liz, we are desperately short of female dice dealers, so if you'd be as kind as to go down to the dice table some of the boys are going to teach you the game," I said. Off she went, she did not even acknowledge what I had just told her, but she headed right down to the craps table. The boys on the game immediately had her paying pass line bets over the other side of the table; this meant poor old Liz had to bend right over and stretch across the table's layout. Within seconds the whole casino erupted into laughter, everybody in the casino had a bird's eye view of Liz's peach of an ass! It is probably the funniest thing I had seen around a dice table up to now, and sure enough made the casino the hottest place to be on this particular cruise. The next day Pled and me were trying to teach Liz how to interact more with the punters. Since all the dealers work for tips it is imperative that all dealers make sure all the guests are welcomed and enjoy their time in the casino. Poor old Liz's English was not too hot, and she struggled to communicate with the punters thus leading to a slightly frosty atmosphere on her games. "Liz, what you need to do is say a few words to encourage the players to smile," I said to her. "What, what words, I do not understand," she replied in her heavy Eastern European accent.

"When a player comes to your table and buys chips to play at your game, you should wink at him, lean over the table slightly, and tell him 'you're gagging for it'," I answered, trying my hardest to keep at straight face.

"Gagging for it? What is this?" she asked inquisitively.

"Oh don't worry, it just means that you're happy to see the player and want him to know that you are here to serve him," I said.

"Oh, OK, gagging?"

"Yes gagging for it," I replied.

Five minutes later Pled and me were watching has some dude walked up to the blackjack table she was on, the dude brought in for £100 and Liz immediately winked at him. The player sat down somewhat bemused and as she passed him his $100 in $5 chips, she bent slightly forward and said, "I'm gagging for it." The look on the players face was worth a million dollars alone. I had tears running down my cheeks for hours afterwards; it was just too fucking funny, and when Liz eventually found out what she had said, she too found the situation highly amusing.

Since the casino knew I would be signing off the ship as soon as my paperwork had been approved to work in Nassau, they demoted me back down to dealer, and promoted Pled up to pit boss. Now Pled is a good lad, but he gets carried away on the booze, I inwardly knew it would all end in tears, especially more so when you took into consideration that Pled now had the signing power in the pit to order himself, and the players as many drinks as they required. On the very first cruise he was the pit boss, he came into the casino looking rather dapper in his tuxedo, hair gelled back and soft scent of brut 33 aftershave. Three hours later, he was lying on the floor in the middle of the fucking pit absolutely wankered, hair all over the place and frothing at the mouth. The ships medical team had to carry him down to his cabin on a stretcher. The manager looked at me, came walking across to my game and asked, "You sure you really want to work in Nassau? Why not stay on here and take back the pit boss position. I will even recommend you for the assistant managers' job. Think about it Windmill, you can have much more fun on here than you're ever going to have in Nassau."

I played with the idea; however, the jungle woman was having none of that, and insisted I signed off as soon as my paper work had been approved. Her argument was

133

quite simple really, she informed me, I would be earning twice has much money on the island, doing the same job. In December 1994 immigration and the gaming board of the Bahamas had finally approved my permits to work in the Crystal Palace Resort and Casino. I would sign off a few weeks early and spend my first Christmas in Nassau. A few weeks later I had a call from Pled in Florida, he had been fired from the ship for being shit-faced in the crew bar and fighting with security, this is what he said: "Alright Windmill, any chance of sorting me a job out in Nassau?" I had to laugh, but somehow could not see him walking into the pit of the Crystal Palace.

NASSAU BAHAMAS

Because of the proximity of the United States and given the fact that gambling was prohibited in the state of Florida, the Bahamas had literally become a magnet for wealthy business people from Miami and beyond. The season, from January to march, coincided with the winter weather experienced in North America. The Bahamians had successfully cornered this market; rich people from the Northern States would flock to Nassau for its guaranteed warm weather, and everything that went with it. In essence, the Bahamas had little or no competition within the region. The driving force behind its economy was the tourist dollars. Most people believed that the Bahamas were indeed located in the Caribbean, but they were not, the islands were actually located in the North Atlantic.

The resort attracted wealth clients very similar to Sun City and they weren't afraid to bet huge wagers in the casino. You had the Mafia from Miami, bullion crooks from Canada, mall owners, mega rich football players' from the NFL, movie stars and time share billionaires constantly in and out of the doors. You could be dealing blackjack to well known mega stars from the world of music one minute, and talking to international movie stars the next. I won't drop any names because I'm not a cunt like that, and don't need to impress any fucker. The dice games were the busiest I have ever known in the season. It was $5 to $5000 the line and five or six times odds behind the line. The games were frenzied, and hundreds of thousands of dollars were being wagered on one roll of the dice. The casino used to hold golf junkets, and all the golfers were craps players. The dreaded junkets were the proving grounds for wannabe dice dealers. If you had the nerve and the skill to battle through a night with these clowns, and still had your head attached to your shoulders at the end of the weekend, you had made it. I will never forget my moment of bliss; I had been at the Palace for a year. The golfers were in town and the fuckers were on a mega roll. The noise they created was deafening and I had lost my voice on the stick. The game was manic, and the golfers were on a feeding frenzy. I looked at the layout and there were chips everywhere, every number, covered in place and come bets. On the eight alone the bets consisted of: spot one, $150 come $750 odds, spot two $2700 place, spot three, $750 come $3750 odds, spot four $30 come $150 odds, spot five $384 place, spot six $990 place, spot seven $180 come $900 odds, spot eight $570 place. The majority of the players' pressed their bets up either in the come, or on the place, every roll. The breaker tapped me off the stick, and I made my way around to second base, adrenalin rushing and head pounding. We had some quality dealers at the palace, and they were all on this game. It was fast, and everything just clicked. Dice dealers know when that moment comes because everything suddenly starts flowing; your hands, movement and mind synchronize. You suddenly have most things worked out before the dice are rolled, and you forcefully get the players betting in a logical order, not just for your benefit, but also for the entire dice crew. Once the crew are in harmonious unity, and everybody is competent and aware of each other's abilities, dice is the be all and end all of casino table games. The same day we went $5 to $5000 the line and 5X odds, one fella bought in for $200,000 one afternoon and cashed out over $1 million twenty minutes later, the owner was not a happy camper at all! If you do not know the casino business, keep the fuck away from it, is all I have to say.

Flem, one of the Bahamian managers thought he ruled the joint with an iron fist. I genuinely liked him though because the man was a real character. Peter Belly, a

legendary dice dealer and me went in for a morning shift at 10 am one day, and there was yet another raging dice game. Unfortunately, I had a fierce hangover from partying the night before and was told by Flem, "White boy, go on third base of that game and slam it." After five minutes of arguments, I reluctantly made my way down the pit. The sticky had obviously been singing – means the dice are rolling without a seven out, because the players were in a state of pandemonium. 'Oh shit,' I thought, this is going to be a fucking nightmare. So I whipped out my 'sun glasses,' put them on, and then tapped out the third base. Five minutes later, it all 'kicked off' because I could hardly see the dice layout.
"Nine winner, front-line winner," roared the sticky over all the noise, and I took the pass line! Flem came steaming down the pit, pushed me into the layout and started ranting and raving. It nearly ended in a punch up because he took one of the ropes that kept the players out of the pit; the fucker was standing near 'Phil's Deli' swinging the thing around his head. The boxman had to hold me back whilst the players were roaring with laughter.

Some geezer from Mexico used to come in every weekend, he was the worst crap player on the planet, over the year he was losing over $3.2 million. He used to get obnoxious towards the dice crews when the roll went bad. I used to hate his horrible attitude when I first arrived there, but I soon learnt that he was actually a nice bloke.

He was a good 'George'- tipper, too, and he would always look after the boys. One night I went in for my shift and he had over $1 million dollars in front of him. "Mate blimey, you have finally won!" I was over the moon, not had he only got most of his money back; he had filled the tip box with black chips. There was over $50,000 in there. Five hours later he was kicking off in the pit, the fucker had lost the lot back! One day this geeky looking American bloke came up to the craps pit, and he brought in for $200. 3½ hours later, he was still rolling the fucking dice. Typically, none of the Palace regular dice players was at the table, and the people playing did not really know the game. After the inevitable seven rolled, the table was only losing $28,000. The casino managers breathed easily, because they knew that if the boys were here, the table would have been down at least several hundred thousand, if not several million. It was the longest roll I had seen.

There were only two casinos in Nassau. The Palace and the Paradise Island Casino. The other casino had been sold and demolished to make way for a brand new resort called Atlantis. Once Atlantis had opened, the resort had taken a lot of business from us. It opened on New Years Eve, and I had been given the day off. I went across to see what the opening of the hotel and casino would be like, and it was simply astonishing. Michael Jackson was just one of the superstars singing outside the hotel, which had cost over a billion dollars to construct. Sol Kezner, the same dude who owned Sun International over in Africa, now owned the place. Many world famous movie stars, and music stars turned up for the hotel's inaugural night. It was the beginning of the end for the crystal place. The hotel and resort could never compete with the newer resort. The guy who owned the Crystal Palace at this time could never compete unless he was willing to pour a substantial amount of money into the joint to bring it up to scratch. Eventually, Atlantis picked off our regular punters one by one until the day arrived when they had all virtually deserted the joint. You cannot blame them either. The new resort was the talk of the international gaming scene. Anybody who is anybody in this world wanted a part of the action. It is similar to being on the red carpet of Cannes or in Hollywood at the Oscars. Just a few decades earlier, the Crystal Palace had captured the world's imagination with its innovation, but now, its time had abruptly come to an end.

We decided to fuck off to Las Vegas for a vacation, but stopped off in Miami for a few nights and had a right result in Cameos Night Club, on Washington Avenue. The owner was one of the punters whom visited the casino in Nassau, so we got the VIP treatment. The next day we were on the way to Vegas. During the flight, we were debating whether to do all that tourist shite, the hover dam, the Grand Canyon, et cetera. The pilot came on the intercom and said, "Ladies and gentleman if you'd care to look out of the left hand window, we shall be passing the Grand Canyon in the next few minutes, thank you." JW and I peered out of the window, looked at each other and said in unison, "Well, we've seen enough of that shit," and then we started laughing and fighting. Well not really fighting, but fucking around fighting. We were both excited, we had worked in casinos for years, Vegas is like a shrine to us people as the Vatican is to Christians.

We did not bother booking any hotels, we never did, and we preferred to hire a car, and then have a look for ourselves. Otherwise, you might be stuck in a shithole and find out there is a better joint up the street for half the money. The first thing that hits you about Vegas is the heat. My gosh it was hot, we were in the middle of summer and the temperature was 124 degrees. However, it is not a sweaty heat as Nassau or Miami is in the summer; it is a dry desert inferno. We rented a car and immediately found a place on the strip just down from Luxor. We then hit the casinos. All the dealers in the various clubs were cool; they knew we worked in the casino business because of the way we played with the chips, like all dealers we stood at the tables spinning chips in our hands, like twats really. We were even offered jobs in a few of them, the Excalibur and Mirage amongst others. Vegas is that crazy you can go and stand in a field of poppies, and Elvis parachutes out of a friggin plane and marries you. Alternatively, you can go through the 'drive through.' "Do you take her to be your wife and would you like a medium fries and coke with that?" Vegas is a great place but ultimately, we both found it a bit too much. They even have slot machines in the shithouse at Mc Donald's. Seven days was plenty and we were not sad when we left, incidentally we had both lost our money, but the experience was well worth it.

Several weeks later in the Crystal Palace something quite peculiar happened. I was dealing a quiet game of craps, and felt odd. The breaker tapped me out so I could take a twenty minute break and, I simply fucked off to the pub. I finally turned up three days later; I was not sure as to what I would say to the management. As soon as I walked into the casino, a manager called Billy called me over, "Oi, Windmill! Come here!" Oh shit I thought, he we go. "Where have you been for the last three days? Everybody has been looking for you?" he said. "Follow me," I replied, and walked towards the exit down by the shops. My mind racing trying to think of the mother of all excuses to dig my way out of the shite I was in. "Billy, I was on the game and I wasn't feeling well at all, scouts honour," I answered.
"And?" replied Billy.
"Well I came out here for a breath of fresh air and you wouldn't believe what happened next." I said, whilst looking up to the heavens.
"Go on," he asked inquisitively.
"Well as I looked up, there was this great big white light shinning down on me," I answered.

"Hold on white boy, are you trying to tell me you were abducted by aliens?" he replied.

"That's exactly what happened," I roared with a grin on my face and disappeared back into the casino sharpish. I still have in my possession one of the finest written warnings in casino history: "Windmill, under no circumstances, is allowed to be abducted by Aliens!" I swear to this day some fucker in the staff room had spiked my rum and coke – yes, you were allowed to drink on your breaks just like the ships. Good excuse though eh?

By this time, the Bahamian and me were not getting along at all, we hardly went out and were forever arguing. It was the end. The brand new car we had brought cost $29,000 dollars and within a year, it had been crashed that much the damage came to $22,000 in that year alone; we were forever crashing the thing. Well there are no drink drive laws in the Bahamas, what did they expect? I remember once been out with an American boxman from the Palace and we had being on a right drinking session out West. On the way back into town we could not remember the way back, anyway, he was shouting, "It's this way," whilst grabbing the steering wheel. I was shouting, "No... It's this way," and a tug of war ensured. A few minutes later the car went up a palm tree on a traffic island. The police turned up with the car still half up way up the tree, with me and my friend hanging out of the fucking thing. Fortunately, I knew the police officers because they had been present at several of my little accidents. "Yo Windmill...I will get the wrecker for ad car man, you wanna ride to da bar?" Welcome to the Bahamas!

The car was back in action a few weeks later, well back in action until Hurricane Hugo showed up on the island. The car would end back up in the repair shop yet again. I only popped out to see what all the commotion was about on West Bay Street. Fucking hell, the strength of the wind had snapped a few palm trees and the things were flying through the air like missiles. Since at the best of times Nassau's streets flooded whenever there was rain, I picked the wrong time to conk out on the live wires that had fallen to earth from the broken electricity posts. I ended up jumping up and down on the roof of the car during the storm. Bad mistake, because now we had no car, well for a day or so anyway.

JW and me had not seen eye to eye on many issues during the previous few months, and the relationship had become tense. Sometimes I wished we could just separate and go our different ways. However, because of the kid we figured the best course of action we must take was simply to try and make things work. Amazing how your best friend one day becomes your enemy the next? Different sides of the same coin I guess.

Back at the Palace, the dice games were still wild. A certain player used to come over from the States most weekends in the season. He was a strange bloke, he only played the do not pass bar. This basically meant he was constantly betting on all the other players to lose their money. The majority of crap players hate these people, and this bloke was the most disliked on the planet. The crazy fucker had a huge gold chain, with a '*Seven Out*' medallion with encrusted diamonds around his neck. Once the dreaded seven had rolled, he would scream at the top of his voice, "That's what I'm talking about!" whilst punching the air with delight. He would also wave his medallion around, blatantly taunting the people who had just lost all their money. Most of the dice crew looked at each other with raised eyebrows, because we knew it would eventually kick off. A few nights later, a wealthy American fella in a wheelchair was on the roll of the century, he kept rolling winner after winner to the roars of delight from the other players around the table. The only person losing, and not cheering was of course medallion man. The more winners that rolled, the more and more his face contorted in inner rage. He finally flipped when our wheel-chaired shooter threw yet another winner. All the players roared, "That's what *we're* talking about!" He could not take the humiliation anymore, and then he suddenly raced around the other end of the table and punched him straight in the face. Within a split second, medallion-man was flat on his back, his teeth laying next him whilst everybody put the boot in. It was hilarious, even one of the bar-servers gave him a slap. Once he regained his composure, the miserable git called the police, and everybody around the table scattered. The police were asking the dice crew if they had seen anything, but of course, nobody had seen a thing.

The relationship with JW around this time had deteriorated further because we were forever arguing over stupid shit. The rows were becoming intolerable, and now the relationship had broken down to such an extent that there was literally nothing left. Everything was at boiling point and in 2001, I told her I was leaving her, and Nassau. The last few years had been crazy man and I needed to get away and clear my head. We just weren't cool anymore, the spark between us had gradually flickered out. That did not last too long either because I had a phone call from the Nassau a few weeks later. jungle woman was pregnant again. There is an old saying that you should never go back and in hindsight, that is exactly what should have happened. However, we had to try, for the children's sake at least. Our second son was born and this briefly this gave us a respite to all the chaos and negativity that had happened. However, it was not long before all the underlying issues of the previous year resurfaced, and the war resumed yet again. This time the eruption was fearsome.

A few nights later things were about to take a turn for the worst because I was summoned to the managers office. My mom called the casino informing one of the bosses that my dad had terminal cancer and that he did not have long to go. In late January of 2001, I left Nassau, this time I felt it might be forever because the situation with Judy had become utterly unbearable. I arrived back home burnt out and absolutely gutted about the situation which now faced me, it was grim. Two weeks after my arrival back home my dad died. I remembered going to see him at Selly Oak hospital and he looked terrible. Cancer is a truly awful condition for anybody to suffer. How it takes hold and distorts a person's physical demeanour is shocking. I had only seen my dad twelve months beforehand, and yet the person in front of me now was virtually unrecognisable.

My dad wrote on a piece of paper asking me what day it was, the ability to use his voice had gone. I responded by telling him that it was a Wednesday. He wrote back saying that he would be dead by Friday. He was right. The strange thing is that my dad was a gambling man; he just loved to have a bet, even though he was crap at winning any of them. This was the only bet he got right in his entire life. RIP Dad.

ENGLAND

Life is a long and twisting road, yet I would never have envisioned all that had happened in my personal and working life up to now. It had been a roller coaster of emotions and ecstasy, of drama and dilemma, one and the same. I assume the effects of leaving the kids, and then the consequence of my dad dying virtually within weeks of my arrival home came home to bear. Leaving a bad situation in the Bahamas to walk into a worse one in England within weeks did not do me any favours. I felt shattered both physically and emotionally. "Fuck this man, you need to get back into work ASAP," I said to myself. Therefore, I swung into action, made a few phone calls and a few days later, I found employment back at the Midland Wheel Casino as an Inspector.

I had only been in the casino a few weeks when an Indian girl nearly half my age tired to move into my mom's house. She was a real nutter, I got a phone call at 5 am in the morning one day and this girl was on the phone crying, saying her boyfriend had thrown her out and she had nowhere to stay. I told her that if she could not find anywhere then she could come over and stay at my mom's house for the night. One hour later a taxi pulled up outside Warwards Lane and she jumped out with all her suitcases. I was gob-smacked, "You've got a lot of stuff for the night haven't you? What have you brought, everything including the kitchen sink?" I asked. She laughed and replied, "Thanks Windmill, I knew you wouldn't mind, I'll only be here for a month or so." My eyes widened and alarm bells immediately began to ring in my head, 'here we go' I thought to myself, 'my old man's just gone to visit never never-land, I've just escaped from a torturous relationship. My mom is constantly going on about Nassau and the boys and now some young Indian girl wants to move in.' It was

147

definitely not the equation I had in mind. Not only that, I'd became cool with another girl in the casino called Dorell, and she'd just left me a note in the staffroom the previous night warning me that this girl had me in her sights. My mom had the shock of her life when she woke up to find suitcases in her living room. She was not happy, not because of the girl, but because of the situation surrounding everybody in the family. She politely told me that the girl had to go. This was quite awkward because I felt pretty bad about the whole thing; the girl was actually a good kid.

Things were becoming more stressful back home already; I had jumped straight out of the proverbial frying pan and straight back into the fire. I really did not want to get involved with anybody, so I decided that working in London could be a real change. For that reason, I went down to the *Sportsman Casino* just off the Edgware Road for a table test on the dice game.

*note: *people who do not deal, or understand the dice game will not understand the following paragraph.*

The geezer doing the test threw me a £1000 chip and said, "£450 each the 6 n 8," "Bet, £100 change, I replied. "Eight, press it by £150, and £150 each the 5 and 9," replied the geezer. I pressed it up, passed him the £75 and placed the 5 and 9. "9, £100 comes," he shouted. I placed the £210 in the come, and handed him the £110. "6, full odds and £200 comes." The joint only offered single odds, so I brought the come bet behind the place bet and proceeded with the action, the 6 pays £525, I took down the original bet, place £100 on the come bet, left £200 in the come and handed him £675. "6," he shouted. I took the come out with the payout, which was £220, brought the £200 come bet in and said, "Full odds?" The guy smiled and said, "Right my son, when do you want to start?" They took me into the managers' office and offered me £24,500 to start. Back at the Midland Wheel, I was on £15,400 at the time. Therefore, in 2001 to be offered nearly 25k to deal dice in London was not too bad.

London is a massive city, and finding a place is relatively easy, the only problem being the cost, which in reality is astronomical the closer you are to the West End. Most people end up renting rooms in somebody's house, in fact through a dealer I knew I had actually secured a room in a flat in Tottenham North London for £350 per month. This is the only real economical way of affording the rents, unless you have millions in the bank of course. The only issue being that I would be living with some bloke, and his wife who I did not even know. I struggled to find suitable place just for myself, which was cheaper than £700 per month, unless it was way out of central London. Even though the casino offered nearly ten grand more in wages, this would ultimately be eaten up in rental payments. The bright lights soon begun to fizzled from my eyes, I certainly would not be any better off financially, simply because of the extortionate price of living in London. Because of family and friends moaning about moving to London, I decided to stay in Birmingham for the time being.

Even though the Midland Wheel had some great staff, and was relatively easy, stepping back into the collective mentality of the English casino industry was not at all. It was worlds away from Sun City in Africa, the Crystal Palace in the Bahamas or the ships for that matter. I now found myself in the remarkable position of actual being bored with the whole casino industry. Only some of the lads in the joint made it worth turning up for work, and one of those lads was Shah. One night in the casino, Shah was inspecting two roulette games, and upon returning from my break, the pit boss said, "Go and take Shah off, and tell him to take a 20 minute break." "Eye eye Capt.," I replied and marched down the pit. "Your break mate, take a 20," I said. Shah gave me the clipboard that followed the players' transactions and replied, "Fuck all happening son, in fact it's all bollocks, I am going to the pub, see you later." I looked at him and smiled. A few minutes later, I caught sight of the fucker in his coat leaving the casino. I started laughing, and asked another lad who was on one of the roulette games, "Is he really going to the fucking pub?"
"Oh yes son, he'll be back in a few hours pissed," he replied laughing. He was not lying either. About an hour and thirty minutes later, he came waltzing into the pit half

pissed. "Where the fucks have you been?" Asked the pit boss. "The fucking pub," replied Shah. From that day forward, I knew Shah and me would be forever mates.

A few months later, I eventually resigned from the Midland Wheel. To be fair I had little choice really, because the management had warned me "If you miss one more shift you will be fired." My mate Dorell, who had the remarkable ability to talk on the phone for marathon sessions of anything up to four hours in one sitting said, "If you do not turn up for work tomorrow, I will knock you out!" At the time, she had been staying over at her granddads house in Handsworth and on the week, we had the same days off she and her daughter Kiesha had come over to stay at our place in Selly Oak. She was good company, and we had a lot in common. "No problem Hanson, when you're ready," I replied.

I had brought an old car as soon as I had originally secured the job at the casino, however, my ex brother in law needed to borrow it on my days off because some fucker had stolen his, which was not a problem because I only used the thing for work. Anyway, the night before I returned to work he called, "Mate, I am so sorry, the gearbox has gone on the car, it is over in Sheldon, how much money you want for it?"
"Don't worry about it mate, it was a lemon anyway, I should have known better than buying a car off my brother," I replied laughing. Therefore, this meant I had to walk down the road, and past the pub to catch the bus into

work. Outside the Brook pub, loads of geezers were singing and shouting, all having a jolly good time. 'Of course,' I thought 'England and Germany are playing tonight.' I could not resist the temptation, and at least they won 5-1. Dorell went berserk, "You fucker, wait until I get my hands on you!" Anyway, she too left the casino few weeks later to get herself strapped in with an estate agent, and I would not hear off her for a good few months.

After a brief spell of doing absolutely fuck all; I decided that I needed to go back to work yet again. The horrifying thought of having no money or signing onto the dole sent shudders up my spine. Why did you not think about that whilst at the Midland Wheel you might ask? Good question, when I have the answer I will upload it in the updates section of this book. I'd half heartedly applied for other jobs outside casinos, but it was proving to be impossible, what other job are going to get where you get paid to go all other the world and get breaks every hour, for twenty minutes? So I applied to work at Stakis Casino, which had recently also been taken over by another group, this time the bingo people, Gala.

I got the job immediately as top inspector. "You will have to come in tomorrow and do your induction," said the manager. "Induction? What do you mean induction," I replied. "Health n Safety," he said smiling. I shrugged my shoulders, left the office and turned up for the induction meeting the next day. What a load of old bollocks that is, for fucks sake, the country was going nuts. Later that evening one of the lads in the pub told me, "The poor old kids have been banned from playing 'conkers' in-case somebody gets hurt." "You are having a fucking laugh aren't you," I said. "Nah mate, you would not believe what has been going on in this country over the last few years," he replied laughing. I had recently watched the news in disbelief when a geezer whom had burgled a house climbed on to the roof. The police turned up, and had the twat cornered, "Come on son, the game is up, give yourself in," shouted the coppers. "Fuck off you bastards," came the reply. Would he come down? Not fucking likely! Several hours later, the idiot demanded that the police fed him, "I want a bucket of KFC and large fries with an apple pie," screamed the thief from his perch. "Regular chicken or spicy?" replied the police. They then proceeded to fetch him his order. Think I am making this shit up? Check out the links on the internet.

All casinos in the UK are governed by an organization called the *Gaming Board of Great Britain*. Now you may have the opinion these people actually know everything there is needed to know about gambling, and the way casino operations run from day to day. Seems perfectly logical? Think again, the majority of them - the board - are actually magistrates whom in reality have no idea whatsoever how casinos function. Simply because they are in privileged positions within society, it is naturally assumed these people hold credible credentials to oversee

153

the compliance procedures of any casino. However, magistrates have no legal rights' they are not trained in law, neither are they qualified, or trained in any aspect of the gaming industry. They are merely elected members' of the public to carry out certain civic duties. Most of them are great people, no denying that at all, but why would government insist on putting a professional body of people in charge of a huge financial business if they had no idea of how that business functions? It seems to this day, bizarre to many within the gaming industry.

This organization was set up in the sixties by government to counter act the criminal element within the business and ultimately make sure, through a rigorous set of rules and regulations, that the business was transparent. This is all fine and dandy, but the problem is that the gaming laws are excessively restrictive. In America, they have a gaming board too; however, anybody whom has been to any of the casinos in Las Vegas will immediately spot the obvious differences with their British counterparts. The major problem with the British gaming board was its reluctance to change, whilst the casinos in foreign cities around the globe offered all sort of lucrative incentives for the prospective gambler to part with his/her hard earned cash, such as free hotel accommodation, free tickets for their shows, free alcoholic drinks at the tables et cetera. British casino owners' could only dream about all of this, because the gaming board would not tolerate it. In reality the casinos in the UK have been subsequently strangled, there would be no free drinks at the tables for the guests, no shows, no promotional incentives, no limousines or private jets waiting to bring in the top players, and definitely no plush hotel rooms for them to check into for the duration of their stays. With the explosion of the internet, the board realized that it would need to change; the original philosophy of its thought was unfounded. Las Vegas had proved beyond all doubt that they fundamentally had most of it wrong, but taking into consideration people who had no idea of how casinos operate in the first place, were placed in charge, what would you expect? In recent years the board is slowly releasing its iron grip on the antiquated rules it set in place, along with its paranoia, but is it too little too late?

The problem all casinos in the UK face today is the emergence of online gaming. This extremely lucrative technology is transforming the way casinos can maximize profits and pay less in taxes. Let me explain briefly how it works. A company can open a casino in, say Latvia, and have a couple of gaming tables: Roulette, Blackjack and Poker. For those familiar with games such as Blackjack you will probably know there are usually seven positions, with seven seats for players to make their wagers. A maximum of three players can play on each position – to the houses maximum wager per position - thus the total number of bets is 7 x 3 which is of course 21.

Now the online casino in Latvia operates in a similar way but with one huge advantage. The player logs onto his / her computer and goes directly to the online casino via live video feeds. The dealers are real, the cards are real and the game is live, however, the rules are slightly different. The amount of players per position is in theory unlimited. Meaning, instead of casino operators hiring huge rooms at premium rental rates in plush parts of cities across the country, they could simply operate from a garden shed to millions.

Roulette operates in exactly the same manner, usually in the UK a player walks up to the game, buys in for cash and receives coloured chips to distinguish his / hers from the other players. Generally, there are a maximum of 8 or 9 colours on a roulette table, but on the internet colours mean nothing. They are all assigned a number, and therefore, the amount of players is in theory infinite. I have personally visited some of these sites and to my astonishment, there were around 500 people playing on one live roulette game alone, furthermore, the computer not the dealer, works out the bets and pays the winning players within seconds. It is nothing short of a revolution.

Back on earth, the Gala Casino seemed OK, same shit different casino. I had only been in the joint for a couple of days when I discovered two fellas from the past were here too. Sooty and Dean Evans were both old school, I had the pleasure of working with both of them in either the USA or South Africa. This is the nature of the casino industry; old faces turn up in the most unexpected of places. "Oi Windmill," shouted Dean. "How's tricks bro," said Sooty with an outstretched hand. The beaming smile upon my face said it all, "What the fuck are you two doing here," I asked laughing. "We were going to ask you the same thing son, last I heard you were in Nassau," replied Dean. "Amazing eh Windy, just seems like last week the three of us were all living in Fort Lauderdale and working the Discovery, and here we all are back in Brum," said Sooty. I agree with that, it had been well over ten years since I had seen either them and although we were obviously older, none of us had really changed. "What you doing Windy, you staying here?" Asked Sooty. "Fuck knows mate, getting a bit pissed off with the business to be honest," I replied. "Why, what's happened?" "I dunno son, just cannot believe we worked all over the world and ended back up here," I said with a certain irony in my voice. "Yeah well, don't worry about that for now, keep your head down and there might be a little something for you in a few months," he replied with a wink.

The management here were actually OK, they suspected I would not be here for too long and would possibly disappear abroad again as soon as a suitable position became available. Dean, the ever profession that he is, ran the pit with the usual military precision that had made him a formidable boss over the years, which bent his teams into shape. Sooty and me were both inspectors, so we just watched the games and pretended we were interested, well I did anyway. Surprisingly, the casino had a few decent punters in who were not afraid to make huge bets. One fella would come in with two plastic carrier bags literally filled to breaking point with cold hard cash. He and his party would stake bets to the maximum on roulette, and if he lost his money, he would disappear for ten minutes and return with two more shopping bags stuffed with more money. We are not talking small change either, anything up to £200,000 would be passed over the table within hours. Whilst working at this club the guy had probably gone through a fair few million in a few months. Later down the years, I heard through the grapevine he had been done for fraud and tax evasion by her majesties finest. How shocking!

You always met a punter you actually liked in any casino, at this joint an Asian guy who had the strangest name of "Mr. Mystery." He was perhaps one of the nicest and weirdest guys I had the fortune to meet in the UK. He had several businesses and several women on the go – or so he claimed, and drank like a fish. I thought he was a spy to be honest, he used to be sitting at the table as calm as can be, then suddenly get up and leg it out of the casino. "Where the fuck is he going?" I would ask. "To the bookies probably." Ten minutes later, he would waltz up the bar, get a drink then shimmy around the casino, hide behind the plastic bushes, then sink back into the chair at the blackjack table. "You OK Mr. Mystery?" "Yes of course I am OK, why? Do I look ill or something," he would reply hesitantly.

"No, no, I was just wondering why...." and then he'd interrupt, "If anybody comes in looking for me, or asking for me, I haven't been here and you haven't seen me." With that he'd wink and slowly slip off his seat without taking his eyes off you, and then he would suddenly turn around and leg it out of the casino. "He's fucking mad he is," said another punter.

Many people ask about cheating in the casinos, and it does go on, there is no denying any of that. The cheats have developed a sophisticated array of methods to try to have you, and the casino in the old net. Perhaps the greatest threat today within the gaming industry is the advancement of computer technology. With all the new equipment available to the criminal underworld, many sharp individuals were making substantial profits from their ingenious devices, and methods to scam the casinos. Certain clubs in London had been hit for colossal amounts of cash; a criminal group had conjured up a remarkable system to edge the bets in their favour. The fraud involved one of the gang standing by a roulette wheel on a live game and secretly filming it on his mobile phone. This signal, transmitted back to an accomplice whom was sitting in a van on the car park, deciphering the information with the aid of computer technology. The software they had developed could predict, through mammoth calculations where the ball would land, literally within five numbers. This information, sent back to another accomplice via a mobile phone; and he would

159

make huge bets on those five predicted numbers. Like all criminals, their downfall was pure greed, as soon as somebody starts to win a lot of money the casinos surveillance department kicks in, and they watch the action intensely. It was not too long before they figured out what was going on, but it was too late. The gang had already taken, illegally, over £8 million pounds from the clubs in London. You will not hear too many people within the casino industry who feel sorry for the casinos, the ingenuity of the gang had effectively made them the "Jack the Ripper's" of the casino world.

The Gala casino did not have the same calibre of piss-heads as the Midland Wheel Club. Some big gay geezer name Matt - who happened to be a Villa fan, seemed all right, and seemed to be the only dealer within the joint to be on a jolly. Well the thing is he was not gay until I pulled a stunt on the fucker. The GM of the casino was an older woman named Carol. She also had a frosty personality and most within the casino steered a wide berth because she was colder than a penguins pecker. Matt, being such a sweety, sent her a loving birthday card and an apple for her birthday, and from that day forward, she would not leave him alone.

"You bastard Windmill, you have stitched me up," he said laughing.

"Why, what have I done?" I replied.

"You know very well what you've done! She only got

one birthday card, and it weren't off me!"

"You will have to pretend you pack fudge son," I said. He was just about to give me a mouthful when Carol came into the pit, ignoring everybody apart from Matt. "Hello, what time do you finish your shift? Would you care to have dinner in the restaurant with me?"

All the casino staff looked on in disbelief whilst he blushed and said, "I would love to, but unfortunately my boyfriend is meeting me down the Jester Pub at 10pm." My eyes widened, her mouth dropped and the whole casino went up in hysterics. The Jester is possibly the most famous bar for faggots in Birmingham.

One night he came bouncing down the stairs to the joint whilst I was making my way up. "Where the fuck are you going?" I asked. "To the fucking pub Windmill! I am day shift, you coming?" I signed in, went into the staffroom and immediately concluded that the boozer would definitely be more interesting. I got my coat and ran past the receptionist heading down the stairs and I heard her shouting, "Where are you going?"

"To the battle cruiser," I shouted. The pub was conveniently located under the casino, Sam Wellers, and within an hour one of the managers called Glen turned up and asked, "Oi Windmill, you're supposed to be on a night shift, it's now 10pm, you were scheduled to start an hour ago, what's going on?"

"I will be up in about another twenty minutes, just got a few more to sink," I replied whilst raising a full pint.

For some strange reason he just shook his head and walked out, no sense of humour some of these fellas I thought. The next shift, and after more written warnings, one of the managers said with a smile on his face, "If you do not conform to company policy, we'll have you chained up in the pit and you'll never be able to piss off to the pub!"

Well blow me down, after a little over two months in this club I was once again back up to my old tricks. After stepping back for a few seconds of quiet contemplation I concluded I actually must be nuts after all. I just could not understand why I would be led astray so easily, why I would consistently get myself into needless trouble. A man of my age now acting like a 17 yr old prick did not make any rational sense. Why couldn't I just be normal like every other fucker? No structure, no concrete plans or goals set in place whatsoever, just a life of chaos. Getting paid, to go and party. Thirty odd years old and still living a life that should have been left behind a long time ago, a life that in reality could never be replicated anyway. Time moves forward, not backwards, and wisdom comes with age, apparently.

Back in the casino Sooty took me aside one night and informed me that he was fucking off back on the ships. He also asked if I would be interested in working for the old firm again.
"What Atlantic Associates?"
"Nah mate, they went under, but Lesley as set up a new

company called Greater Atlantic if you're interested in working for us?" Of course, I was interested, and Sooty offered the carrot on the stick of which I could hardly refuse.

"You dealt heavy dice games in Nassau didn't you?"

"Yes mate, why?" I replied.

"Well there will be a position open for you out of Tampa Florida as a boxman on the dice game if you're interested. Give it some thought and let me know by tomorrow," he said. My mind had been made up instantaneously, Sooty knew I had two kids in Nassau, and he also knew I would not turn down the offer.

I left Gala and got myself ready to return to the Florida sunshine. Two weeks before I was due to depart; I had a call from the office state-side asking me if it would be possible, I could join a ship out of Venice Italy called The Olympic Explorer. The rep in the office said a situation had arisen and they desperately needed somebody to join the ship that weekend. She also assured me that it would be only for a few weeks and then I would revert to my original destination of Florida. I could hardly refuse, after all, the office had always looked after me in the past, so I had no reason to doubt their motives.

EUROPE

Flying to other European destinations from the UK is a bonus really because no country is more than few hours flying time, and since I absolutely hate flying the less

time spent sitting in a tin can the better. This was my first time in southern Europe and Venice was breathtaking. Even the short trip from the airport to the dock was interesting because some of the stunning villas lining the streets. Many had impressive statues looking down from the roofs, overlooking and blessing the properties.
I absolutely adore things like this, it shows a remarkable belief of what this country was in the past, and what through its philosophy, gave the world. All inscribed in the Latin language. *'domine nos degere,'* one proclaimed with angels sculpted in marble. The port was very impressive, a bee hive of activity with people shouting and running around excitedly. Venice is a city quite unlike anything within Europe, a kaleidoscope of human endeavours culminating in all the magnificence we have today, an achievement of excellence.

The ship, the Olympic Explorer, was in reality a converted Greek trooper carrier; she had initially been designed for the fast deployment of troops in case of unrest, doubtless with the sovereign dispute between Greece and Turkey on the island of Cyprus. She had been recently refitted and converted into a liner, but she was fast, probably the fastest cruise ship in the world. I could not believe my eyes when I walked into the casino pit for my first shift though, Sooty was the manager. He had personally requested my placement with him on his ship, I had been swindled. "You git, I thought you told me that you were going on a ship out in the Pacific?' I said to him. "Nah mate, whatever made you think that? I asked the boss to put you on here so that I can keep an eye on you," he replied whilst laughing. Now it suddenly dawned on me the call from the office had been a load of bollocks and Sooty had requested me on the Explorer.

"OK Sooty, I must admit you've conned me on this one, but they said that I'd be only on here for a few weeks, so what's the real deal?" I enquired.

"Mate, a few weeks? They must have given you the wrong information son, because you are going to do a whole contract on here, just to make sure you behave yourself and then, we can talk about a ship out of Florida," he replied. I had already informed my eldest son that I would be in Florida shortly, now he was going to think that I was a bullshitter. I laughed, but to be honest was slightly disappointed.

Regardless of the fact Sooty had pulled off a con-trick, the real bonus of working on the Explorer were the magnificent ports the ship visited. The Aegean Sea is spectacular, the sight of the Greek Islands' rising as temples out of the mist can only be described as stunning. You can really see why these ancient islands have given inspiration to countless artists and philosophers over the centuries. *'Sailors' spread their sails, to the winds tempted so rarely, the affluent earth gave way to the deep blue sea...'* it's the place of dreams, of deeply rooted poetical love. Homer was the teacher, the Achaeans' listened spellbound and later so did the rest of the world.

Europe is the continent which has everything. From the magnificent fjords up in Norway to the Temple of the Gods' in Athens.

We docked in the ancient port of Athens, Piraeus, and the assistant manager insisted that I went out on the lash with him. "Mate, I'm not really here to go on the lash, let's head up to the Acropolis in Athens and make a day of it," I said. Stevie was having none of that though and insisted we had at least one drink in a crazy bar he knew. Well it would not be polite and not sample the local brew, so off we went for a few scoops. The bar was one of the strangest I had had the pleasure to visit so far on my travels; it was a mixture between a brothel for the sailors, and a hardcore drinking den.

"Right, I'll order the drinks, you grab a table by on the Avenue", said Steve. You could write a best seller about the sort of people in here, a right mixture of scallywags and cut-throats of all nationalities. It was like something out of the wild west, 'any minute now it's going to kick off,' I thought, and I was not wrong. Suddenly one of the tarts who worked the bar smashed a bottle of something over some fuckers head, "You bastard," she screamed, but nobody took any notice. The geezer staggered to his feet and then she let him have it: a quick jab to the stomach and a left hook. The poor fella went hurtling backwards crashing onto another table knocked clean out, it was hilarious. "Don't fuck with her," said Steve, whom by this time had returned with the drinks.

"Why, what the hell is going on", I asked.

"That geezer is the owner of the bar, and the bird who has just knocked him out is his missus," said Steve.

"No fucking shit," I retorted, I could not believe what I had just seen. I enquired what drinks we had, and Steve informed me that this was the best whiskey bar in Piraeus. I had a swift gulp and nearly fell off my chair.

"For fucks sake mate, how much whiskey have they put in there?" I asked. Steve just laughed. I am not joking either, the amount of alcohol dispensed in this tall glass was unlike any bar I had ever visited. I found this out when I went to get some more drinks, I watched in disbelief as the woman behind the bar literally filled our glasses to the top with whiskey and then added a 'splash' of coca cola. 'Holy shite', I thought, this could be dangerous, I was already swaying on my feet after the first one, no wonder everybody in the bar was shit faced. A few hours and several drinks later I was on top of the bar singing, fighting with the other sailor's, and kissing some of the slappers. I cannot even remember what happened to Steve, but I figured I'd fuck off back to the ship, but I did not make the gangway.

I decided to take a 'short cut' across a traffic island, and promptly fell backwards in the middle of it, crashed to the earth and fell asleep. Sometime later, a Greek woman was slapping me around the face, trying to wake me up. My mind was completely in disarray. I partially opened my eyes, which were completely out of focus, to see a pretty face in front of mine. Her lips were moving, but I could not hear a word she was saying. Everything was in slow motion, and then her voice suddenly reached my ears, "Hey malakas, are you OK?" she asked.

"Where am I?" I answered, ever so casually.

"You're in Piraeus señor!" she replied with a beaming smile.

"I know that… sorry, I do not mean to be rude, what time it is please?" I replied.

"It's nearly ten minutes past six señor….why?" she asked. My world crumbled, the blasted ship was due to sail at six! In addition, whilst I had taken a 'power nap,' some git had taken off my trainers and nicked my fucking socks. I jumped to my feet to see the Explorer pulling away from her berth; I had missed the ship. It definitely was not the equation I had in mind. I had to go and see the port agent and he arranged for me to stay in a hotel over night. I had to fly to the island of Corfu the next day, I knew Sooty would be raging, but what had happened to Steve. Had he been nicked? Was he still on the piss? I had absolutely no idea. I was rather embarrassing arriving at the airport because I had only been on the ship a week, and already managed to miss the bloody thing. It was not the first time either, because I managed to miss the MV Atlantic in Nassau in 1994 and got an ear full from the staff captain and a twenty-dollar fine. I was not at all sure what would happen this time, actually missing a ship is frowned upon and ultimately can lead to instant dismissal.

I knew the people in the office back in Miami would be raging though, it would be a foregone conclusion that she would give me a right 'ear roasting.'

I arrived on the island of Corfu absolutely broke and I had no idea how far the port was from the airport, the only option available was to walk, however far it was to the ship. Luckily, for me the port was only four or five miles, so it was easily within walking distance. As things turned out, I am actually glad that I missed the ship, because Corfu is beautiful. Not only was the arrival into the Greek Islands' stunning, the actual places themselves were equally impressive. The walk to the port took a little over two hours, I was in no hurry either because you can get a real feel for the way these people conducted their lives by this little excursion.

The Greeks are very friendly and ultimately I felt very much at home here. It was strangely like walking into the past, the rustic buildings painted in differently lightly coloured pastel shades, the impeccable deep blue sky and the soft breeze whispering through the olive groves. My journey took me past countless properties where the inhabitants were causally having afternoon lunch in their gardens. These scenes my eyes witnessed probably happened every day, loving and enjoying each other's company with some delicious food and wine. You certainly would not have an opportunity to view these scenes on a package holiday. So the episode of missing the ship had in fact been well worth it, well in strange sort of way.

Eventually I made it to the harbour in Corfu, the walk had cheered me up no ends, regardless of what Sooty was going to say, he would not be able to diminish that fact. I made my way up the gangway and immediately went straight to the casino; all the staff was in there because they were having a meeting. Sooty was not fucking happy though, I could tell by the look on his face, all the other fuckers were laughing their heads off though.
"Fuck me, it's Robinson Crusoe!" shouted one of the lads, and all the others burst out laughing. I was surprised to see Stevie sitting sheepishly in the corner, head slightly bowed. He did not say a word, I think Sooty must have given him a right roasting, and knowing Sooty he'd probably put all the blame on Stevie for my misadventures.

Surprisingly, Sooty hardly said a word about the sorry episode and casually just brushed it off, as if nothing had happened. Maybe he felt bad about bullshitting me in the beginning about this ship. My days were numbered on the explorer though; I think I lasted about two more weeks and I resigned. I did not want to be here, even though I loved the ports of call, we were working shit loads of hours and to be honest my head was somewhere else. We eventually made our way to Istanbul for an overnight, and I can honestly say Istanbul too is a great city. The clash of civilizations have taken place in this

extraordinary city for thousands of years, and not only
that, they serve up the best lobster on the planet.

We eventually retuned to Venice calling at Mykonos and
Santorini in the Greek Islands' on the way back.

Those two islands are equally as impressive as Corfu.

The next cruise out of Venice we called at Dubrovnik in
Croatia before making our way to Bari in Italy. Both these
ports were excellent too and seeing old world Europe was
in essence brilliant, but not necessarily right for me at this
particular time.

So one night I got wankered with my cabin mate -a
cockney geezer whom could lift up one of his eyebrows
like James Bond, and we drank about two bottles of rum
each and partied all night long. The following morning
Sooty was banging on the cabin door informing us that
we had yet another hated sea day.

"Oi, you two, open door, it's a sea day and both of you
are due in now!" screamed sooty from outside the cabin
door. "Not today Sooty" I shouted, "yeah," said Bondy
boy. After much squabbling at the door we eventually let
Sooty into the cabin, he did not look too happy either.
"What is going on with you two? You are both need to be
in the casino within the next twenty minutes,"he said.
"Sooty, mate I'm not going into the casino... fuck this
shit, I'm not working ninety hours a week for $500, I
resign," I replied. Poor old Sooty looked in shock, "But,
but you can't say that Windmill, what about the kids in
Nassau? I said to you if you behave on this ship then you

can go on the next contract," he replied.

"Sooty, sorry mate but to be honest you know I shouldn't have been on here in the first place," I said slightly agitated. Sooty and I spent the next twenty minutes or so in fierce debate, but I would not move one bit. My mind already made up; I was to sign off in Venice in two days time. The next day I went to his cabin and explained all to him, Sooty understood.

"Windmill I have known you a long time and you aren't thinking right at all mate, you need to get a grip and come back to reality," he said.

"Yeah, tell me about it son, I cannot even begin to tell you what is going on, but don't worry. Listen, I did not have the intention to come on here and fuck you around mate, just keep that thought." He had been a good mate over the years and in no way was it a reflection on him. I know I had let him down in reality because he had firstly secured the job for me in the first place, and then I had missed the ship within a couple of weeks. On the dock on the day I signed back off the ship he came up to and said, "You're mad Windmill, you're going back to England to what? The Gala? This might be hard work, it might be shit but it is better than working in any casino in Birmingham mate, you know that." We shook hands, and I jumped into a cab.

So here I was again, sitting in some airport contemplating the philosophy of life, or something like that. What the fuck was I going to do now? I had hardly sat down and worked out a master plan. In fact, I had no fucking plans. It appeared to me that my behaviour was becoming even more irrational. I was constantly walking out of casinos and obviously, I was not happy. Sitting on the plane flying north-west to England I began wondering if the constant boozing had anything to do with it all. The inner demons, the dark recesses of the mind overtaking rational thoughts and making me behave in an irrational and repetitive manner. As the plane landed on the tarmac of Birmingham airport I suddenly felt nervous, "fuck, the family ain't gonna be happy to see me back home already," I said under my breath.

My mom went ballistic when the cab pulled up outside the family home, "Do not tell me you've walked off the ship already? What is wrong with you? I thought you were going so that you could see the boys, and now yet again you have no job?" Of course, she was right. It was pointless arguing with her because I simply had no logical defence. "Well you had better get yourself sorted out soon, because you have made enough money over the years to take care of yourself. I cannot just keep worrying about you all the time; I am selling the house and moving to a retirement apartment." She suggested that I find employment immediately and sort out a mortgage so that I could move onto the property ladder.
"Mom, don't worry about me, all that matters in this life is your happiness. You have had enough shit to deal with over the years, now it is your time to go out and enjoy

yourself, I will be fine," I replied smiling.

"I do not know why you like those bloody casinos anyway, it seems to me ever since you first came back from the ships all those years ago you had acquired a taste for the drink," she said.

Looking back on the extraordinary events just a few days previously over in Venice Italy, you would be forgiven for thinking, "He'll either get a job in Birmingham, or fuck off to London," well think again. Remarkably, I decided to book a flight to the USA and find employment on one of the gambling ships running out of the port of Miami. Now considering I had just walked off a ship and the fact if I had stayed with the company and finished my contract I was guaranteed a job in Tampa, it was madness. I will not even bother writing down what my mom said about it all, however, I will say she said, "Once you go, you had better make sure you do not mess up, because the house is sold, and you will not be able to stay at the new place."

"Mom, do not worry, I know what I am doing," I replied. A few days later I arrived in Miami and took the shuttle down to Dollar rent a car. Whilst driving across the causeway to South Beach I glimpsed across to all the ships docked inn the port, I smiled because being back in Miami in some ways was like coming home. I had spent so much time here in my life, by either working or visiting whilst living in the Bahamas, I knew the city like the back of my hand. However, this time things did not go to plan. Since I had last worked on the ships there, they had changed the law. Like I have said previously, you could just turn up in Miami; walk into one of the cruise ship companies' offices and get a job. Not so anymore, you had to apply for any position from your native country, so I was screwed. To my horror, I had not done my homework because now every company I visited insisted I would be offered a position immediately; however, I could only apply from England. This would take at least a month or so to sort out because of the paperwork, therefore, I had dropped the clanger of all clangers.

On the plane back to the UK, my mind went into overdrive, what the fuck was I going to do now? The hostess came around and said, "Would you like a drink sir?" I looked up at her, a radiant olive beauty with sparkling eyes, "Yes, just leave the trolley," I replied. She learnt forward and replied, "Are you OK, sir? You look agitated."
"No, I am fine, just a bit of self inflicted stress. Can I have a couple of large whiskies please, and a coke," I asked smiling.
"Certainly," she replied and proceeded to pour a couple of miniature bottles into a cup of ice.
"Are you staying in London," she asked.
I looked up and replied, "Are you?

SOFA SURFER

Once I arrived back in Birmingham I really did not know what to do, or who to call. I checked into a hotel on the Hagley Rd and paid for a room for a week so that I could figure out a way of pulling myself out of this unprecedented situation. I daren't call my mom and tell her the "good news." Money was an issue, because my bank account was running down to the few hundred and in this city, it was not going to last long at all. I called my brother, "Oi, what is happening son."

"Alright kid, where are ya? The Bahamas or Miami Beach?" he replied.

"Erm, no mate not exactly." For a few seconds there was a deafening silence on the line, and he then said, "The line seems rather clear, usually when you call from the USA there is an echo on the line... you're in fucking Birmingham aren't you?" He said.

After explaining to him what happened, he came around immediately to the hotel to have a word.

"You are going to have to go down the council and see if you can get a joint ASAP. You can get a job in any casino, but you know you only get paid at the end of the month so you're fucked," he said.

"The council? Fuck that, I ain't going to any council," I replied.

"You have no choice mate, all your mates have families and they aren't going to put you up, I cannot because the house is full and mom can't because she only has a one bedroom flat."

Having very few options, I went to the council enquiring about the possibility of acquiring one of their properties immediately. The woman in the office informed me straight away, "None are available, and you will need to put my name on the housing list."
"Really and how long does all this take," I enquired.
"The process of receiving an offer for a property can take up to two years," she said.
My face dropped. I then noticed an asylum seeker who was gleefully accepting a set of keys to his new home.
"Tell me, how do these people get immediate assistance?" I asked. She smiled and said, "The council has an obligation to house them."
This shocked me for a moment, and then I asked her, "Do you think that man has paid any form of tax or national insurance contributions towards this country?"
"No comment, it is all to do with legislation in Westminster," she replied with a grin on her face.
I was not laughing though, talk about a sharp kick in the family heirlooms.
"So do I, as a British citizen, have any options available during these extremely difficult times?" I asked.
"Yes of course you do, you can move into a hostel," she replied. I learnt forward, my eyes drew tighter together and I looked at her intently, "A hostel? Are you serious? Aren't they places for backpackers?" The woman giggled.

For fucks sake, the bloke who just jumped off the banana boat is the fucking backpacker here, and he gets a joint whilst they want to ship me into a place probably written in the hitch-hikes guide to the galaxy.

Anyway, I managed to do a bit of Sofa Surfing here there and every fucking where and after six weeks, I had managed to get the funds together and I moved to the suburb Moseley in Birmingham and stayed there for around 14 months on College Road. One of the geezers living in the apartment below seemed like a decent sort of fellow, much older than me, yet very intelligent. After we made our initial acquaintance we became friends, Philly boy had an interesting story behind his life too. His father was once the chief pathologist in Birmingham and his had links to the aristocracy over in Wales. Very posh spoken and obviously from not around this neck of the woods. So there is always a catch isn't there?
"Tell me Phil, how on earth have you ended up in Moseley in Birmingham?" I asked.
"Well, it is quite a long story, and it is something I really do not like discussing, however, during my university days I read chemistry. A chum of mine on the same course suggested we manufacture amphetamines with the view to supply South Wales. Reluctantly I went along with the plan simply because my mind was inquisitive enough to see if we could actually produce the substance. Unfortunately, we indeed managed to produce the rotten stuff, but we were caught in an undercover sting after a tip

off to the police. In our possession were nearly four kilos of the blasted stuff, and trial judge did not take too kindly to our exploits. I received seven years of hell at her Majesty's Pleasure in various prisons across the land, and eventually ended up here in Birmingham at Winson Green. My family basically disowned me because of their social standing in the community. My father has passed away now, and he never really forgave me for my stupidity. My mother has only really started conversing during the last year or so. Therefore, a promising career and all my hopes went with that prison sentence. When they released me, they put me into temporary accommodation right here in Birmingham. At first, I was reluctant to return to Wales, but after a few years, I went back. It never worked, and I drifted from one place to the next, and ended back in Birmingham, and I have lived here alone now for almost twelve years."

I was stunned, and here I was sitting listening to all this thinking, fuck me Windmill, and you thought you'd had a rough ride! Anyway a few weeks later Philly boy managed to talk me into starting an Open University course. This I thought might give me an opportunity to gain a degree or two, it was impossible to get a job without one these days. Therefore, if I really wanted to break away from the casino industry, I definitely needed more education. I chose a mixture of history and Language studies for starters and lasted around eight months, talk about a drop out. I believe the professor Mr

Rolleston didn't appreciate me turning up to his tutorials shit-faced, well what did expect if they put a pub next to the Open University centre in Harborne? I absolutely loved the language studies though; it is pragmatic, pragmaticus and pragmatikos. I still speak in fragmented Latin to this very day: Windmillius stercus facies semper est quod verberat nos et lacerat fortuna! Loosely translated this means, 'Fortune always beats us because Windmill is always shit faced'. Since I was unemployed, I could get a computer from the University. Things were certainly going to change with the arrival of that piece of kit. The first thing I managed to do was set up an account with William Hills, the bookies. Well on a purely academic perspective, I could monitor the horse-racing. *Professor Plum* and *Hoof Hearted* were running that very afternoon at Cheltenham. At least I could navigate my way around a familiar environment such as the virtual betting shop. If they had a pub online, I would have gone there first. Being new to computers, it is only natural for you to 'study' something that you know. I certainly got the drift of it very quickly and within a few weeks, I had it all down to a tee. Philly boy filled me in on the more technical issues that arose and things were going extremely smoothly. Then one day everything was about to change.

I returned from the boozer one night pissed up and played live blackjack online. I won around £312 within an hour and decided to cash in the £300, and play around on

Poker with the shrapnel. I made a bet on Caribbean Stud Poker and received, Ace, 1, 2, 3 and 4 of spades. I had a straight flush. I also had a £1 in the progressive jackpot box; the jackpot was £127,500 quid. I received 10% of that total, £12,750 quid for a £2 initial layout. I went downstairs to tell Philly boy that I had won £1275 quid playing Poker.

"Are you sure Windmill, you look rather the worst for ware to me, hold on, let me come upstairs and have a look for you," he replied.

"Bloody hell Windmill, you have won more than that; more like twelve and a half grand!" said Philly boy.

I was ecstatic, I could not believe it, suddenly everything had changed and I suddenly had quite a substantial amount of money in my sky-rocket.

I paid off all my debts and decided to go to the Bahamas to see the boys' and give them some monies. Once back on the island it felt strange going back to Nassau as a tourist, renting a car and staying in a hotel. It was even more surreal going around to Crabby Street to see the gang. I was not sure how jungle woman was going to react, but it was something that needed to be done. I had not seen the boys for three years, Ash since he was one. The three of us were in a state of absolute euphoria when we finally hooked up again.

Seeing the jungle woman was strange too, we were both slightly hesitant but ultimately everything was OK but we both understood the bigger picture for here and

181

now and both remained cool. That week in Nassau went so quickly it was like a blur, the greatest aspect was that I was actually back for Ash's Fourth Birthday and I made sure he had a birthday he would not forget. I also spent a small fortune, probably to the tune of $7000 overall trip, but it was well worth it. Leaving Nassau again was a strange feeling, the boys came to the airport and we said our farewells, little Ash broke off running and tried to come on the plane back to England with me, we had bonded superbly and it was hard leaving him again.

After paying off all my debts and after going into a dodgy business with my brother, I was nearly broke again within a year. The experience of our little adventure was well worth the effort though. Our business took us all over England, to classic car and motorcycle shows. We were selling anything and everything you can think of. One day we were working in a beautiful and huge stately home, Knebworth in the southern England. The previous week, we had done a deal for 200 motorcycle jackets with some geezers in London. Foolishly, we had not bothered to check the merchandise. When we got them out the van at Knebworth, we realised that they were all size S. Given the fact that most bikers are fat bastards, we would have virtually no chance of flogging them. Que the fucking Pikey's we met at the stately home. "Top of the mornin to yer boyz," said one of the travellers. Twenty minutes later, my brother and I had sold the lot for double the money we had originally paid for them. We had taken two motorcycles and a few hundred quid in the deal too. Later that day, after a superb day of trading, we went to see our pikey mates. The poor fuckers had not sold one single jacket, and they were fighting amongst themselves. It all went wrong a few weeks later, because we had done yet another dodgy deal. This time though, we went bust.

I decided I really needed to get a real job. Poncing about in fields the length and breadth of England, regardless of the fun I was having, was not getting me anywhere financially. The only option I really had was back in the casinos. One of my old boxman from Nassau called from Miami, he was now large and in charge for NCL and he offered me a job as a supervisor/boxman. I initially declined the offer because of the shit on the Explorer. He reassured me that the casinos within his fleet never worked anything like 80/90 hours a week. Yeah right! I believed him, and I signed on The Norwegian Dawn in Dover England. Consequently, I was fired three weeks later with another geezer from Birmingham for failing a breath test. We were working all the hours god could send, and it was three or four to a cabin. I called the boss in Miami and told him I was in Helsinki. "Wow, have a great time there Windmill, are you going to the Senaatintori market?" he replied.
"No mate, I'm going to the fucking airport. I thought you said 'you won't be working a zillion hours a week,' and I have been fired anyway for getting wankered in the crew bar, see ya!" and I hung up. The only good thing about the

whole experience, I managed to roll around with some half-French/black girl from the Seychelles.

So I turned up at the China Palace Casino on Hurst Street in the city centre and asked for a job, surprisingly they agreed and I was to start the very next week. The casino was a bit shit, bad atmosphere about the whole place. Did I really care? I just wanted to do my job and go home. Dorell and I were still cool and she came to stay over in Moseley on a few occasions, she too needed another job because things had gone pair shaped at her other place. Therefore, she turned up at the Palace, not that she actually liked the place -she thought the place to be a shithole, and she wasn't wrong either. We both ended up fucking off to Rome together for a vacation. In reality I should not have gone, because I promised the boys I would be back for Ash's fifth Birthday. The vacation was not what we expected it to be. We stayed in a hotel in the Cornelius suburb of Roma. After checking in, we excitedly made our way to the restaurant to savour the authentic taste of Italia. We sat down in the quiet dining room and ordered the food. Five minutes later the waiter returned with two frozen packets of Findus spaghetti and asked, "How would you like it cooked." Words failed us, we were literally gob-smacked, and it left a sour taste in our mouths. Indeed, it was a taste of things to come because of some serious issues with the Romans themselves. Rome is full of tossers these days; they gave Dorell a hard time because everybody thought she was a prostitute. Unfortunately, many of the black girls in central Rome work as hookers, and because she was with me they obviously thought the worst, it was exceptionally depressing. Everywhere we went people were staring at her with obvious disapproval. The saddest thing is Dorell is a beautiful girl and it visibly made her very sad.

We had never seen anything like it; well actually, I had in South Africa many years previously. We made the best of a bad situation though and we nearly were nicked in the Vatican when Dorell tried to climb over the barriers so that she could go and meet the Pope, and ask him why his citizens' were being wankers. We also went to Florence and at least there, the people gave Dorell the respect she deserved. The damage had already been done though, and we could not wait to return to Magna Britannia. Dorell found out after we arrived back that she was up the duff from her an old fling. This was awkward for her and she did not know what to do. I bumped into her on the way to work, she looked ashen faced, "Mate, what's up? Why the long face", I asked her.

"Its twins Windmill…" I told her I would give her a call later, but it was obvious that there could be no turning back now. Dorell eventually left the casino after a few more weeks, she could not hack it, I did not blame her either and I told her that I too would be out very soon. Back at work, I was barely turning up for shifts - yet again.

The GM at the Palace knew I was talking the piss but because of my experience and given the fact that the joint was so short staffed they could not, or would not fire me. This isn't really funny to be honest, I was just finding extremely hard to keep myself out of the pub. Another GM turned up because they were about to spend several million pounds transforming the club and changing its name. The China Palace had a bad name since several triads had stabbed a bloke to death in the bar a few years previously. The new GM took a shine to me because I had been around the block and knew some of his mates, in fact a geezer from Nassau and the cruise ships came in one day, Thomas Oliver. A great bloke who I thought was in Miami running Costa Cruises for Carnival. It turned out that he married a dancer and moved to Scotland and had become a manager up there. He seemed happy and I was happy for him, quality geezer. Anyway, Harry, the new GM wanted me to go and work with him in some casinos he was setting up and I told him I would definitely be up for the position.

But before that happened my old mate Shah had got a job with Royal Caribbean and was joining a ship in Southampton. He asked me to go down with him, naturally I'd never miss an opportunity to go on the lash-especially with the old school, so off we went. The ship was actually a Celebrity ship, which was a parent company of Royal Caribbean. We went aboard and some geezer in the casino shouted over, "Oi Windmill is that

186

you," I looked around to see a fellow I had not seen for over a decade. It was that twat of a boxman from the Pacific Star, all those years ago which sailed out of San Diego. "Oh, hi Spocky, what the hell you doing on here," I said frostily. Fucking hell I thought, can you believe it, the twat has not changed in twelve years and here he is on here. Shah whispered in my ear, "Who's that cunt," and I informed him that was exactly what he was. Shah did not look happy, but I told him to chill because twelve years is a long time and the bellend might have changed. Anyway, I was offered a job immediately with Royal and they said they would be in touch within the next few days to sort out a position if I was interested, of course, I said I might be. I had heard through the grapevine that Royal was considered one of the only good shipping companies left. However, even they themselves were not much better than the others were. Nevertheless, they had a few ships that only engaged in three and four-day cruises, so this meant there were no sea days. One of the ships was located out of Miami and visited Nassau twice a week. Given the fact that my experience of dice was very good, I was in a good position to request whatever ship I desired, as long as I behaved myself on my first contract. Shah asked me what I was going to do; I had already made up my mind I would be definitely working for RCCL. I told him of my plans and I told Shah to behave himself and not get his ass fired. "Shah, keep your fucking head down son and I will see you in few weeks;

Shah are you listening? Keep out of the fucking crew bar," I said. The only reply I managed to get from him was a solitary "Yeah," and he and the ship were gone.

Everything was falling into place, the casino in Birmingham was due to close in two weeks time and everybody had a month off whilst they made the casino over. RCCL had already been on the phone and informed me that I was due to sail on The Legend of the Seas, out of Southampton to Tampa Florida. I only told a select few of the boys at the Palace that I was heading off back on the ships, they all kept quiet about the affair, and the management was none the wiser. My family was making noise though, as they always did, especially my mom. I had viewed some apartments in the city and I even left a deposit on one I was supposed to be buying, one of those half buy half rent things. She kicked up a right stink about it. I told her that there was no way on this earth I was going to get myself into a position where I'd be financially crippled by taking on that responsibility. Why should I stay and work in a place that paid poor money and then struggle with a mortgage and everything else just to make ends meet?

I snaked my way down to Southampton to join Royal Caribbean's Legend of the Sea's in October 2005. Stu Reading was large and in charge of the casino department over in Miami, he had been around the block and warned me before I joined, "It's not like the bad old days of AA, the ships have changed drastically, and you won't like it."

I had already prepared myself for all the bollocks, the plan was to try to keep my head down and put up with all the bullshit. Well that was the plan anyway, whether or not it was actually going to work is another matter; there is a massive difference between theory and practice. I only had to sail across the Atlantic to find that out with that twat Shah.

We arrived in the port of San Juan in Puerto Rico ten days after leaving Southampton, this was a good time to call the old fucker and find out if everything was going OK. The American Cell number he had given prior to my departure on the Legend was dead. 'Uh oh,' I thought this sounds like trouble. So instinctively I called his old mobile number back in good old blighty.

"Hello? The phone answered immediately, it was Shah.

"Oi numbnuts what the hell are you doing in blighty? As the ship turned around and gone back? What the fuck is going on son," I asked.

"Erm, I got the nine ten jack, son."

"You what? You have been fired already, I do not believe you, what the fuck have you been doing now?"

"Well let me tell you…I was in the crew bar and…"

"Hold on hold on my son, what did I say to you before you left? I said keep out of the crew bar, for god's sake Shah, you've been on the ship less than one month, "I got into a fight…."

"You were fighting in the crew bar too? I don't fucking believe you mate, I really don't. Shah I'll call you later," and then I hung up. Inwardly I was laughing because it was 'vintage Shah,' the fucker is forever chinning some twat. Now that meant I would not be able to see him in Tampa or wangle it with Stu to put us both on the same ship. Everything was going pear shaped already because there is no way Royal would allow him back for scrapping in the crew bar either.

The legend was OK. There was more English staff on the ship than I thought would be, so you know there was always a party to crash or a beer up for grabs. My cabin mate on here was a geezer called Nicolas Numbnuts the First. The dice game was only $200 maximum the line and single odds, even the slot techs could deal it like a champion. Talking about slot technicians, one of them had been promoted to casino manager; he could press a six dollar eight like a pro!

Me and some of the lads were always on the lash in either Costa Maya in Mexico or Grand Cayman in the Caribbean. It was a good ship to work on and we had lots of fun on and off board. Me and Gazza – one of the dealers, became good mates on the ship, and had plenty of laughs off the fucking thing too.
"We're in Mexico tomorrow Windmill, what's your plans son?" asked Gazza in the crew bar on night.
"Well, we're off, and you know Mexico is famous for the tequila," I replied.
"A few margaritas and a few señoritas sounds like a plan." The ship had actually gone to Cozumel for this

particular cruise, the place was major tourist attraction and had plenty of bars and restaurants to explore. The next morning we were ship shape and Bristol fashion and ready for some action in Mexico. Cozumel is OK, it's a party town full of people out to have some fun, mainly college kids from the USA on spring break. We spent all day lashing it up, yet nothing of great significance happened until we went around to the local knocking shop. We did not go around to employ the services of the girls, we were curious to see what the totty on offer was like because we'd heard back on the ship some of the girls, were actually lady-boys. One of the tarts on the door had a pair of stockings on, a pair of high heels, and 'she' was sporting a huge curly wig; however, the tattoos and the stubble on the chin gave it all away. Me and my mate looked at each other, laughed and decided to make a hasty retreat. The pair of us had already had a skin full, yet it was pretty obvious the thing on the door was no Mexican princess. We decided to hot the famous No Name Bar and catch up with the rest of the ships company before hitting the beach. "Gazza, try and behave yourself in here mate, no ten pinters," I said laughing.

Back in the UK when a group of lads are out for the night, you can bet your bottom dollar one of the boys will end up with a 'ten pint princess.' This terminology is given to any girl who looks gorgeous after ten pints of beer. Usually the next morning one of the boys will be on his phone to his best mate, "Fuck me Harry, you ain't going to believe it mate. I must have been really wankered last night, there's a ten pinter in my bed."

Back on the ship, some of the older hands waited eagerly for new hires to sign on the ship and, they went to extraordinary lengths devising new schemes to fool them. One fellow had been watching the brutal American prison series OZ during his contract, and it gave him some new ammunition to use against the newbies. A few weeks later whilst docked in Tampa Florida, we had several English new hires sign on the ship. After a few days, one of them was asking us what was life really like onboard the ship. Davor – the old guy with the OZ series said, "We have the Filipino Mafia, the Peruvian Mafia, the Yardage Mafia, and so-forth." The new fellow believed him too, "Really?" he said, "You mean there are actual gangs on the ship?" Davor nodded, and told him that he should get himself a shank because it could be dangerous below decks. The new guy fell for everything Davor said and it was now becoming hysterical. Later that day in the casino, I was tapped out for a break. The new fella - Mark, was standing on a dead blackjack game and whilst passing him I whispered in his ear, "The Peruvians are going to make a move; they want protection money from you." He came rushing into the staff mess ashen faced ten minutes later. "What do they want? Why are they picking on me?" he asked. Davor also came into the mess, he sat down with us and said, "Listen, you need protection. You must join a gang on the ship, otherwise everybody is going to shake you down." I sat there trying desperately not to laugh. Davor also said, "Windmill and I are members of the Aryan brotherhood." We both raised a clenched fist. "Do you want to join?" I asked.

"Yes, yes of course! What do I have to do?" replied Mark. "Every time you walk into the mess, or the crew bar, just raise your clenched fist and everybody will know that you're a brother," Davor replied. For the next minute, the three of us were sitting in the mess holding up clenched fists to the amusement of other departments on the ship. "See, they all know now you're a brother Mark. Nobody is going to fuck with you," said Davor. We were telling the casino manager later, howling with fits laughter whilst Mark was walking all over the ship with a clenched fist. Later that evening I got one of the Peruvian dealers from the casino to call Mark's cabin and demand protection money. He came rushing around to see Davor and me, and asked what he should do. "If he calls again tell him the brothers will 'shank' him on the I-95 if he tries anything," I said. We had all sorts of things planned for the poor boy, but unfortunately, the casino manager went and told him. Mark later told us that he actually believed everything we had told him, and that he'd also bought a machete in Tampa! Mark later said he should have known something was up the very day he signed onto the ship. Apparently, one of the officers gave him a life-jacket and told him to go on the top deck for "Iceberg Watch." Considering we were in Tampa Florida heading for

Central America the chance of seeing an iceberg would be rather remote. I remember some other dealer saying to another new hire, "You know why there are so many portholes by the waterline don't you?" The new hire said, "No why?" "Well if the engines decide to pack up half way across the Atlantic Ocean, we all have to start rowing; if you look under your bed in your cabin you'll find a hoar."

The first contract with RCCL went extremely quickly and, a few weeks before I signed off we had some excellent players onboard who literally filled the tip boxes with $100 chips for the dealers virtually every night. During a ten-day spell, the casino dealers on the Legend had made over $4500 in tips each. I had some more good news too, because I was informed prior to my vacation that I would be joining the Majesty of the Seas.

I went back to England for eight weeks, I had nowhere to stay and in the beginning, it was an absolute nightmare. Even after sending thousands of dollars in Nassau to ensure the boys' education, I still arrived in England with around ten large. My mate Dorell wanted me to stay with her, but there was just not enough room. Fortunately, I managed to rent an apartment for my brief stay back in England. This was tricky really, because many companies wanted you to sign a six-month rental contract, which for me was impossible. However, some Indian girl sorted me out with a quiet place above a shop in King's Heath Birmingham for as long as I needed it, and without any contract to sign. The vacation was uneventful really; I just needed some quite time to chill. I wasn't getting any younger so the partying was put on ice for this holiday. However, whilst staying in this flat I had a run in with some wanker who lived next door, which would have massive implications later down the years. I will get to this later in the book. My superstar mate Dorell was good, she had to give birth to two twins and she was happy has Larry - whoever he is. I went to see her and the children and brought them some gifts back from Miami.

We also went on the lash one night to reminisce about philosophical issues such as life etc. "So sir Pedro, tell me my dear, what business plans do have in mind to make a quick buck," She asked. "Well Dorellus, what do you think of these bad boys," I answered and produced two diamond rings. "Holy shit, are they real?" she asked. "Of course they're real. I can get them at a knock down price too," I replied. "I reckon if people here show an interest, and I can flog em fast enough, then maybe me and you can become international diamond dealers." Dorell was still looking at the diamonds, and asked, "How much do you reckon they're worth, and more importantly, why are they just men's rings, and why isn't one in my size?" "Fuck off, I knew if I'd brought over a ladies ring, that would be the last I ever saw of it, or you," I answered laughing. Anyway I tried to flog one of them but because of the economical downturn in the country, the price I could get was not that much more than I'd actually paid for it, so decided to hold on to the assets for a later date when the market was a bit more buoyant. As if I sound like I know what I am talking about! I also went down to London to see Gazza and fat-boy Derek from the Legend, this turned out to be an expensive night. We all went to the casino and initially, I was winning. I bet £700 on seven boxes of Blackjack and won them all, only to lose the lot back playing Roulette later. Nevertheless, we had a jolly good time and leaned a very important lesson in life; never ever go to London to see those pair again!

A few weeks later and I was back on the plane. Being back in Miami was bliss, there is always something endearing about the place, its vest and vibrancy is always contagious. The Majesty was the crème de la crème for casino dealers because it had no sea days. For me it was a tremendous step forward because the ship would be in Nassau every Sunday and Tuesday, I would be seeing both the boys twice a week for the next six months. I joined the ship on a Friday and quickly settled into my work. Surprisingly, quite a few of the casino crew were British and there seemed to be some decent people onboard. The casino was in reality a sideshow though; I was not interested in all the parties these days, I was here to see the youngsters. On Sunday morning the ship pulled into Nassau harbour, I must have been the very first person off the ship, in fact I believe I was off even before they had finished tying up the ropes! I went straight to a phone box on the dock and called Crabby Street.

"Hello can I speak with Al please," I said to the maid who had answered the phone.

"Hello?" he said, "Yo Al what..." I was interrupted, "Windmill? Is that you? Are you here…" he replied.

"Bad news mate, the ship will not be docking in Nassau until next week," I said.

"No, don't say that man, dad…" I interrupted Al this time and said, "Look mate, I really have to go, there are two people waiting here to use the phone and the ship sails in five minutes, I'll call you".

"Dad hold on…." then I hung up, trying not to laugh. I immediately ran out of the dock and caught a cab directly to Crabby Street; five minutes later, I was outside the door. All pandemonium broke out when I went rushing into the house, Al nearly fainted, and Ash was jumping around like a six-week-old springbok. It was hilarious, the boys were obviously very happy that I had finally come back. Following the initial greetings I could see something was bothering the elder one, I could tell something was not quite right.

Because I had been away, I had no real idea of what was actually happening in Nassau, I definitely could not rely on any concrete information from anybody within the immediate family. To see the truth, you had to see it with your own eyes. I could see that by looking into my eldest sons face; but I needed more information. Al told me that things were pretty tough and his mom had gone slightly nuts, she was constantly moaning at him for no reason.

"Welcome to the club son, now you know exactly how I'd been feeling for the last few years!" JW was not actually around here on the first day, she had moved into an apartment. I only had a short time here on that particular Sunday because I had to go and do those stupid sign on meetings all new crew have to go through. Ten minutes later jungle woman's sister Stella came whizzing around the corner in her car, she looked shocked to see me. We had a brief discussion and she immediately called JW to inform her of my arrival. The ensuing conversation I had with her was brief too, she initially moaned because I had not called her to tell her of my imminent arrival. She come racing around the corner half an hour later, obviously looking for a fight. Al was right, she did look fucking nuts, "Yo jungle woman, what's up," I said. "Don't you call me jungle woman, why the fuck haven't I heard from you in the last year?" she shouted, slightly agitated. I somehow managed to calm the fruit bat down a bit, and told her I had to leave. However, I informed her that the ship would indeed be back on the Tuesday, and she said she would be around then. I took Al to one side and gave him all the money I had in my pocket, I instructed him to order pizza for him and Ash and that he should go across to the gas station and get some sodas. I inwardly knew though things were going to be tricky back in Nassau, so the best course of action would be to avoid her at all costs.

The best thing about the Majesty was that it had no dreaded sea days. This alone made a tremendous difference to the casino employees lifestyle. The money was good too considering all the competition in Miami, so everybody who worked for RCCL in the casinos either wanted to work on the Majesty or another ship of similar calibre out of California. Even though the Majesty was relatively easy, all the new rules and regulations were making things difficult. Whilst in port you now had: elevator duty, fire duty and welcome aboard duty. In other words, you have very little time off the ship whilst in port, and this was only going to get worse. Back in the 1990s, the cruise companies done something that would change the cruise ships forever.

All ships that visit ports pay port fees per passenger. I do not know the exact figures these days, but back in the 1990s, for a ship to dock in the port of Nassau it was something like £10/15 per head, plus other fees. Carnival Cruise Lines had several ships which visited the Bahamas virtually every day, and the revenues generated for the Bahamian economy were significant. During renegotiation of the yearly fees, the Bahamians wanted a substantial increase on docking fees; however, Carnival used their corporate might to barter a deal more favourable to the cruise ships, rather than Nassau. They basically told them they expected no increase in port charges, and demanded their ships were allowed to open the casinos in port; otherwise, they'd pull all ships from the Bahamas. This was disastrous for the Bahamians because not only did the revenues generated from the port fees' contribute to their coffers, the passengers on the ships were crucial for their tourism generated economy. Carnival had become a huge corporation that dominated the cruise industry, and they knew the government of the Bahamas could not refuse their demands. Once the Bahamians gave in to their demands and the casinos were permitted to open whilst in port, many of the casino staff resigned. They did not see the point of working onboard any ship if you had to now work whilst tied up in the harbour. Furthermore, since all ships had bars, restaurants and nightclubs already onboard the ships, many passengers simply went to the beaches during the day, and stayed on the ship at night. Consequently, this has had a disastrous effect on Nassau. All the famous bars are no more. The legendary Drop Off pub closed a few years ago. Overnight the cruise company had destroyed the once bustling nightlife of Nassau harbour. If any sailors of yesteryear remembers the days when there were five or six ships in port at 5am in the morning, with thousands of people milling around, they would be shocked today. The harbour and down-town area now resembles a ghost town at midnight on a Saturday night. Needless to say, I was absolutely shocked to see what had happened to Nassau in just a decade.

Back to the Majesty, one cruise we headed down to Jamaica for the Christmas period, and a few of us hit a bar in Ocho Rios. Jamaica is a pretty cool island. I have been to most of them in the Caribbean over the years, and can honestly say, "if you've been to one, you've been to them all," meaning there is little difference between Barbados or St Lucia. Sunshine and smiles, crime and destitution. During the 1990s ships actually stopped visiting Jamaica because the tourists kept getting robbed whilst on excursions to various tourist traps located around the island. What many people who visit these islands fail to realise is the chronic unemployment and poverty hidden away from the plush beaches and swanky hotels. It is a massive issue in the Caribbean, and the authorities on every island try and hide the true statistics of the problems because tourism is the only real industry, which drives the economy of the whole region. Once this is damaged, the consequences for the average man on the beach is grim. It took a substantial amount of time for Jamaica to regain the trust of the cruise liners, and now Nassau is suffering a similar disposition because crime against tourists is becoming more frequent.

This was virtually unheard whilst I lived on the island, and goes to show how things can change so quickly. I doubt the crime issue on Nassau will ever reach a point where the ships will avoid the port. There are several compelling reasons for this. One, Nassau is the closest, developed port to Miami - meaning the ships save fuel by visiting her port; and two, the new ships are nothing but floating cities. They can keep the passengers happy by visiting in the morning and pulling out before the sun sets. This is what actually happens these days. Over nights are nothing but a thing of the past for the majority of ships. They cost so much to construct and, there is so much competition, it is necessary to keep them out at sea - meaning the guests spend their euros or dollars onboard, and not on the islands. Now it may become more clear having explained previously the dire situation with the long gone nightlife of down town Nassau.

I was sitting on the back deck of the Majesty in 2008, just like I'd sat here on the Majestic back in 1990, thinking of all these changes in such a relatively short period of time. How I left the Atlantic in 1993 in this very port, to go and work at the Crystal Palace Casino around the bay, and how over the course of the next few years all my old ships mates had resigned because they refused to work whilst in port. The extraordinary events with JW and, the madness associated with the casino industry.

A new supervisor signed on in Miami, a crazy fucker from Hungary, and he turned out to be a riot. Zolton had a zany personality and was open to a bit of persuasion. One Saturday night Able and I were in the pit, he was dealing Roulette and I was dealing Blackjack. A new assistant manager had signed on a few weeks previously and he was a real company boy. The fucker would not close the casino, even if there was only a few punters left in the joint playing the slot machines. Anyway, Mark the manager had taken a night off, so that left Zolton and this

202

other geezer running the casino. At 11-45 in the evening, the assistant informed Zolton that he was going up to the midnight buffet for some nosebag.

"Oi, Zolton come here," I shouted across to the podium. Able instinctively looked over with a grin on his face.

"Yes Windmill, what is it?" enquired Zolty.

"I hope you realize that Mark has purposely taken the night off so that he can monitor your management skills whilst he is away," I answered.

"What, what do you mean?" asked Zolton.

"Well, Mark likes his supervisors' to use their initiative and try and get the casino wrapped up by 12 midnight," I replied.

"Really? He likes the casino closed early?" asked the Hungarian, with a puzzled look on his face.

"He has informed Windmill and me that he thinks you have the potential to step up to management, but firstly, he wants to know how you will run the operation," shouted Able. Immediately after our conversation, Zolton grabbed the microphone and said: "ladies and gentleman, thank you very much for your patronage this evening, and let me inform you that casino royale will be closing in approximately 30 minutes time, enjoy you day in Nassau tomorrow."

The casino was packed, and all the other dealers stopped what they were doing, and looked at Zolton in disbelief. Able and me could not believe he had done it either, and we immediately burst out laughing. Twenty-five minutes later, lee the assistant manger returned from the buffet to find half the tables empty, and a huge queue at the cashier's desk. He marched up to Zolton and asked, "What the fuck is going on? Why are all the guests leaving?" Zolton looked at him in a calm and controlled manner and replied, "I have used my initiative and called it." "What do you mean you've called it, it is only 11.55? We do not close the casino until 3-00am? You'd better uncall it, if you know what is good for you," screamed Lee. Zolton wasn't having any of that, he just turned his back and walked off. Tears of laughter were streaming down our faces by now. Zolton would not budge, he insisted that he had done the right thing and instantly he had become a legend in the annuals of casino staff.

Able and I went back into the Crystal Palace Casino one day to see if any of our old mates were still there. We were stunned to see the transformation. When we worked at the joint, the casino had literally hundreds of staff and loads of gaming tables. Within a short few years of Atlantis opening, it had collapsed. There were no more than five gaming tables open and what few staff remained, worked just one or two shifts a week for a few dollars per shift. Many people had been hit financially very hard because they had taken out big mortgages when the times were good. Now, many of them had lost not only their livelihoods, but also their homes, it was exceptionally sad to see, and hear. The positives being that the Palace would be demolished and rebuilt by a consortium of Chinese businessman who were about to pour in around three billion dollars to completely rebuild the whole strip on West Bay St.

Back on the ship, the cheapskates were still hard at work. The next cruise, one of the male passengers embarked the ship with a fucking toolbox hidden in his luggage. Apparently, with the soul intention of looking into the AC unit in his cabin to see if there was any dust in the duct. One of the pursers later told us in the crew bar, "This man came charging down to the reception with a digital camera and a screwdriver in his hand, screaming and shouting that the ship was unhygienic, and that he had a good chance of catching Legionnaires disease." Everybody in the crew bar howled with laughter, I had witnessed, and I had heard of some of the shenanigans the passengers had been up to, but this really was the crème de la crème. He did not even bother staying for the cruise, and immediately signed off the ship. His purpose was simply to find a way to visit his lawyer and screw the company with a lawsuit. This was becoming an all too familiar occurrence with the various cruise companies, and the passengers were going to extraordinary lengths to squeeze a few million dollars out of the cruise ships. Every cruise company had an army of lawyers' to deal with the never-ending devious motives of the public.

One of the lads in the casino asked me what I had planned on my vacation. I had been arguing with the Bahamian on New Providence the previous cruise, and said that I wanted to get a boat and sail across the Atlantic. The thought must have stuck in my mind because in Key West I called a geezer and enquired about sailing lessons. As things turned out this were a brilliant adventure, not only did it break up the monotony of working on the ship, it would give a break from Nassau. Better things were to come, because I actually began to get involved, and the geezer teaching the course was a fucking riot.

KEY WEST

Captain Dave is real character man, he once owned *Southern Most Sailing*, in Key West Florida. The geezer is a natural scallywag; I bet he has shagged more women than Ron Jeremy. He drinks hard and parties hard, yet he loves being on the ocean. Forget films like 'Pyrates of the Caribbean,' the real deal is right in southern Florida. Several of the lads from the casino were interested in taking the course, including the manager George Furlong. He was OK, he had been on the ships for over three hundred years, and he too was sick and tired of some of the bullshit that happened on them these days, "I preferred the olden days when the ships were made of wood," he said. "What with a few hundred slaves rowing too?" I replied. Sailing is an art, it is more complicated than you think, but mainly it involves the basic human commodity usually known as common fucking sense.

The captain turned up with a couple of strippers on one outing and it was hard to focus on the job in hand. How are you supposed to 'watch your heading' when some stripper is in her g-string, bent over the bow throwing her ring up? "You fucking limeys are supposed to be natural sailors eh? Well stop fucking watching their asses and Tack, heading 35°," said Dave, who should practice what he fucking well preaches, because if we set that particular course, we would have ended up on the rocks!
"What reach are we on Windmill?" enquired the skipper. Reach, the only reach I had in mind was to reach over to the bow and grab a handful of that peach of an ass that was pointing in my direction. Sweet Jesus, what a sight, it was like a full moon. "Erm, we are on a…broad reach I think; but fuck all that, I am heading up!" I shouted. The captain just let out a roar of laughter, and I quickly passed the helm to one of the boys and made my way forward.

One of our casino boys was a real calamity; the fucker wasn't adapted for the seafaring life at all. If you looked up the definition of a landlubber, this guy was your man. He eventually dropped out of the course, presumably for his own safety. He managed to break a toe one week, and then somehow got stuck up the mast the next. Whilst conducting a man overboard drill for the exams, we had a real man overboard emergency because this twat managed to fall over the side when the boat rolled in the swell. The final straw came for Captain Dave a week later, the bloke got his leg trapped in the genny line - a rope that holds a sail, and nearly snapped his leg off. He too said that one day he fancied sailing across the Atlantic to England; however, Dave told him, "Forget it mate... you won't make it past the buoys of Miami harbor."

We took these lessons every Thursday; I also went sailing on the the ships private island in the Bahamas nearly every Wednesday and Saturday, and I loved it. These lessons continued for the best part of two years and out of all the drop outs, and people who did not get fired, only George and me passed the sailing course. I only have to do another 200 hours on the fucking water and I can put in for my captain's license. That's right, captains, so if you happen to be on the water and see some 'black sails' heading your way, it will be yours truly.

Key West is a brilliant place; it is so laid back and very cool. There are loads of bikers down there and one day I heard a familiar 'trumpet sound.' Like I mentioned way back in this book, I brought a Triumph Tiger Cub. The bike was twenty-two years old and I was seventeen. Sure enough, the bike making that sound was a Triumph and some other geezer was on a BSA. They pulled up outside *Sloppy Joe's Bar* so I went over to have a chat. I noticed that the BSA was a three cylinder Rocket. I remembered the Bob telling Nobby and me all those years ago on the plane over to South Africa that his old man used to take him to school on a rocket. I said to the geezer that my mate in England used to own one, he looked puzzled and said, "That's not possible man, the 68 Rocket was built for the American market only." I smiled…

The contract went very quickly because of dealing with the boys in Nassau and all the sailing on the other days, plus the shopping days in Miami. There was no chance of me sailing across the Atlantic just yet. Therefore, I did not intend to go back to England for my vacation. Fuck that, the American dollar was not worth shit in the UK at that time, and I certainly was not going to lose half of my hard-earned cash to 'exchange rates.' Therefore, I had the brightest of bright ideas and decided to fly to Cuba for my vacation. I was not confident enough to sail down there, knowing me I would probably do a Columbus and end up in Greenland or somewhere completely off course.

The company had already arranged a ticket to fly back to the UK because it is the the Law of the United States that crew signing off must depart to their homeland. I got around this by signing off in Nassau a few days before we were due to dock in Miami. I stayed in a hotel in Nassau, the Holiday Inn on West Bay Street. It was OK, I was only there for a day, and I had not told anybody in Nassau of my dastardly plans. The next day made my way to the airport for the flight to Havana; the flight was less than two hours, so I was ready for action. It was strange thinking about Cuba, with all the political and economic strife the country had suffered during its difficult existence. The real reason I was heading for Cuba was a purely financial one. I only had a little over $2000, and this must last the entire six weeks, I had not even paid for a hotel. Therefore, I would literally be living from day to day, or so I thought. On the plane I met some Irish girls who were on working in Cuba, they gave me all the information I needed about the place, and the best hotel to stay in considering my circumstances.

We arrived in Cuba shortly afterwards, I was excited because there was a lot of taboo surrounding the place, with all that communist bollocks. The trip through the suburbs and entrance to the city brought me back to reality though. I looked out of the window gob-smacked; the place was a real shithole. It was worse than Russia back in the early nineties. Everything appeared derelict and dirty; the whole country appeared to be caught up in some surreal time warp. My subconscious was already going into overdrive, questioning the viability of being here. The people looked decimated, scruffy, and lost. The buildings echoed this dilemma; it was thoroughly shocking to witness it at first hand.

The hotel was located in a side street, which was so run down, you could have actually believed there had been a recent war here, and everybody had deserted it. However, if you looked closely, you could see people in the shadows of the windowless windows. I had been too many countries, and seen a lot of poverty on my travels, but this was unprecedented. I knew immediately that I would not enjoy my time here, that I had in fact made a huge mistake. I arrived at the entrance to the hotel, opened the lobby door, and stepped into a completely different world. The air-conditioned lobby's appearance did not conform to the chaos and deprivation outside. That brief transition from street to reception, comparable to stepping off a space capsule.

All the hotels in Havana are owned and managed by the state; so naturally, they have a strong desire to keep them in good standards. The US dollar is not the common denominator anymore, the Cubans' much preferred the Euro, which is stronger and therefore worth more to them. After the brief shock of my arrival, I proceeded to the check in counter. A sweet Cuban beauty, with a beaming smile and a massive pair of jugs, took down my particulars. She was rather too friendly, and I immediately suspected that there would something more on offer than just the room. She informed me that she could not accept American dollars, well not for the room anyway. She told me to head down the street and exchange them into Cuban Convertibles, the local tourist currency. So I headed out into the unknown, not sure of what to expect, apart from deprivation. I walked down the rundown street with great caution, better be safe than sorry I thought. To be fair, the locals hardly gave me a second glance. Even so, it was instantaneously obvious that these poor people were living in utter poverty. They looked under-fed and desperate. I eventually found the exchange place, done the business and made a beeline for the hotel. On the way back, several women offered their services for what amounted to little over $10. I declined the offer, not because I was not particularly interested, but because I had over two grand in my pocket. Better be careful I thought.

My charming little Cuban host greeted me with her infectious smile upon my return to the Lido. After seeing what it was actually like outside, I was not at this point sure if I was going to be staying here for six weeks. Therefore, I took the diplomatic option and paid for three nights only. This would give me enough time to venture into central Havana itself, to check out the other joints. The cash exchanged, the deal done. Gloria handed me the keys, and held my hand for the fleeting moment, you can always tell what a woman wants by the look in her eyes. I smiled, and I presumed I would be seeing her later. The room was very basic compared to the lobby. I presumed that this hotel room would be worlds away to the squalor the locals were dwelling in, but it was bog standard compared to western hotels. It was two-thirty in the afternoon, so I decided that I would take my camera and checkout the local sights, to see what was cooking. I wondered if the legendary Copacabana Club was in the vicinity, I really wanted to shake a leg in there.

I wasn't surprised at all by central Havana; the place was exactly like the rest of it. Derelict old Colonial buildings that were well past there sell by date. They needed demolishing; the place was a real shithole man.

The poor old Cubans were driving around in nineteen fifties cars, it was like something off a film set. Some people might think of such a place romantic, fuck all that shit, the place is a living museum. The only problem is that the caretaker as pissed off and nobody as bothered to sweep or clean the place up. You cannot blame the locals though, the real reason Cuba looks the way it does today is all down to political ideology. The embargo set by the USA has had a tremendously devastating effect upon a whole nation; it is a real human catastrophe. On the other hand, it becomes immediately apparent that there is hardly any American influence on the island what so ever. Compared to all the other islands in the region, Cuba has retained her own identity, regardless of how painful that may be.

I managed to find a bar and found the prices of the grog to be mightily favourable. In fact, a beer was less than a $1, 'I'm in heaven,' I thought. The main street was bustling with both locals and tourists. Given their predicament, the locals seemed happy and content; maybe they were happy to be living under the iron grip of Castro. I got chatting to some German's who were here looking for a bit of bum fun. It struck me as rather peculiar that all the Germans I'd ever had the misfortune of meeting, were indeed 'sausage jockeys.' I made my excuses and headed down to the harbour, to see what sort of entertainment would be on offer. I managed to find another bar -I have an uncanny knack of doing that, and ordered some of the local cuisine. This turned out to be a rather dismal offering of a piece of rotten fish in salsa sauce, combined with a few grains of rice and a warm cup of brownish looking water. Saying that, for $2, what do you expect? 'Well, time to go back to the Lido, and check out Gloria,' I thought, and made my way back through the bustling streets to my briefly adopted 'humble abode.'

I arrived back at the hotel a little after 5pm, and my smiling princess was still at her station. She gave me a wave, pointed upwards; presumably meaning my room, and flashed her fingers like a star four times. I nodded instantaneously; I took it that she actually meant that she would be upstairs in twenty minutes. Several of the boys whom I had once worked in the Bahamas with, told me that the Cuban girls could not get goods like; shampoo, deodorant, conditioner, hairspray, skin cream or any other toiletries that women take for granted in the west. So all the boys from the Bahamas came to Havana with suitcases full of the stuff, and they were guaranteed all the 'services' the girls had on offer; for a bar of soap here, and a bottle of shampoo there. Therefore, I dived into the shower, had a shave, and opened my suitcase to put on fresh clothes; it took awhile to find the fuckers though, I had so much shampoo and hairspray in there, I could hardly find anything!

Once you become a sailor, it is traditional to have a Motto. Mine is, 'Any port in a storm' it has a philosophical issue to it, I apply it at 6am every morning if there are only 'old hags' left in the bars or nightclubs I am in. Since I was now in Cuba, and it was nowhere near 6pm, I decided to go for the classical Latino look: a pair of khaki shorts with sandals and a crisp short-sleeved shirt. I glanced at my watch, unlocked the door, and dived onto the bed, soap in one hand, and shampoo in the other, waiting for the arrival of my Cuban cutie. Sure enough, at the exact time she had mentioned, there was knock on the door. "Come in", I shouted in excitement.

"Señor Windmill is there anything you need from room service?" said a big fat horrible troll of a woman with no teeth. "Yes, can you please send me up the pus…I mean, can I please see menu", I replied rather embarrassingly.

"Se señor," said the large one, and then she had disappeared. That is rather strange I thought, I wonder what had happened to my Gloria. Exactly one minute later, there was another rap on the door, by this time I was taking a slash. "Just drop it on the bed for me darling, I'm just having myself a good old fashioned piss," I said.

I came out of the bedroom expecting to find a menu on the bed; I found something a lot tastier than that, it was Gloria. "Wow, I am sorry, I thought you were the maid," I said with embarrassment.

"That is OK señor Windmill, do you not mind me lying here, I is tired very much..." replied the beauty.

Do I mind? Is she fucking nuts? Of course, I do not bloody well mind, now get out of those clothes you poor thing and go and have a nice hot shower. Oh, and here, I have brought you some shampoo; these thoughts ran riot in my mind. "No absolutely not, you rest. Erm would you like to take a nice hot shower. I should imagine you are very hot and sweaty after a hard day's work, ooh fancy that, it appears I have brought some women's toiletries by mistake, of course I could sell them to you?" I said eager to get down to the real business. I was not thinking straight, what the fuck was I talking about, 'I could sell them you.' I thought I might have blown it there and then, but to my utter surprise, she whipped her kit off and was straight in the shower, dragging me behind her, yee ahh! It is amazing what a bit of barter gets you these days, for a few bars of soap and some hairspray; I was having it away with a gorgeous receptionist in my hotel room within a few hours, beat that boys!

I know a lot of my mates, especially the fucking birds back home would be saying in their winy fucking voices, "ooh you shouldn't be doing that, you're taking advantage of the poor girls," et cetera. Fuck off it is business mate, welcome to real world. It is free enterprise, the girl was demanding something and I was supplying it; the only difference is that money did not exchange hands. Only hot breath and a few hours roll around in the sheets!
Now I know why Cuba was so popular with all the boys in Nassau. Anyway, the gorgeous Gloria 'thanked me' for my services, and retreated from my room with a couple of bottles of shampoo and a bar of soap. I remember sitting on the edge of the bed chuckling to myself, thinking of

the girls back in England. Imagine if it were that simple back there, walking into a nightclub with a suitcase full of Tesco's home brand shampoo and having a bevy of beauties surrounding you, and offering their services...nah!

Several hours later I went down to the bar in the lobby, Gloria had long gone. I was sitting there sipping on a rum n coke wondering how many of these 'transactions' took place each day. The funny thing is I was expecting her to ask for some money too, but she did not. Even when I offered to give her a few bucks, she declined. She was happy enough to have that stuff women love so much, cock. I think she liked me, because she warned me of the women who roam the streets outside, she told me to be extremely careful because there was an upsurge in crime recently. I should have heeded her advice because the next night I was fucked. The next day I decided to get on with all the tourist rubbish, stand here, stand there, have your photo taken and all that malarkey. I was approached on several occasions by some dodgy looking ho's, offering their services for a pittance. I declined on every occasion because they simply looked like proper mingers. I also started to feel slightly uneasy about being in Havana, especially on my own because there were many Europeans here. Big fat pervy types looking for some fun, the problem with that is you do not really know what sort of fun they are looking for, and some of the people gave me the creeps. I also felt slightly paranoid; I felt that all the Cubans thought I was here for the same thing too. I remember some bird on the Majesty, Scooby; she asked me if I wanted to go to Thailand with her once, I said I could not go there because I would not want the local people looking at me like I'm some sort of fucking nonce. Anyway, I did all the tourist crap, and I still was not impressed with Cuba at all. The place was an absolute shithole as far as I was concerned, it was worse than being at Villa Park. I could not bear the thought of being stuck here listening to all those 'Spanish twats' trying their hardest to sell you everything they had, including their daughters, or even sons for much longer. I should imagine that back before the embargo, Havana would have been a fantastic place to visit, sadly, those days have long gone.

I arrived back at the hotel around nine o'clock, and headed straight for 'man's natural habitat,' the fucking bar. I sat quietly on my lonesome and knocked back several large rum n cokes. Later that evening, I decided that I needed something to eat. I asked the barman if there were any pizza parlours open. He told me that there was one several blocks down the street, so I decided to try it. I wobbled off in the direction I had been given, and surprisingly, I managed to find the joint. I stayed briefly and eat my food with a few cold beers, then decided to head back for the night. Once I got outside though I could not remember the direction I had came from, it all looked similar. I thought I had come down a hill, so naturally, I followed that path, but within a few minutes I was obvious I was lost. There were shadows on every corner. One girl came across to me and enquired if I required her services, I declined. I did ask her to give me directions to the Lido hotel though; I even said to her that I would pay her $5 to show me the way. She happily agreed and took me by the arm and led me in the opposite direction. I never suspected anything, not a thing.

We turned a corner and I noticed several people hanging around under a street lamp. We passed them, but she seemed to give them a signal and, before I knew what was happening, somebody had grabbed me around the neck. Men appeared from nowhere and I was on the floor. They rifled through my pockets in a matter of seconds, hands everywhere. My camera, my money, and even the cross from around my neck were gone in seconds, and so were they. I jumped to my feet stunned; they were already 100 yards down the road, running for their lives. A police officer appeared from nowhere and gave chase. Then I realised the awful truth, I had all my money in my pocket, they had taken everything. I was now fucked, proper fucked. Luckily, if you can call it that, in the haste to get away quickly they had dropped one of my $100 bills, how fucking thoughtful of the wankers. I felt stupid really, because Gloria had warned me about the possible dangers, but when you've had a few scoops you seem to let reasoned thought go out the window, well I do anyway.

There was no point going to see the coppers, fuck that I thought, so I just went back to the hotel. I had already decided that I was going to get out of Cuba in the morning. I still had a ticket to fly to England; I just needed to get to Miami within the next 36 hours. The next morning I checked out, I was furious that I had been stupid enough to go out in the middle of the night, half pissed, and get myself mugged. I immediately got a cab and went to the airport. This turned out to be a joke too; the stoned faced immigration tosser sitting behind his little plastic protective screen was taking forever.

"Señor what was business in Havana?" he asked without lifting his ugly mug. "Tourist..." I replied coldly.

"What you come to our beautiful island for just over a day?" he retorted.

"Well some of the people on your beautiful island are wankers," I shot back.

"What is wanker?" he asked.

"Go look in the mirror," I retorted.

At that point, I believe I pissed off good ole Carlos, because a few of his fellow twats came across and took me to a private room. As things panned out, the fuckers thought I was a British spy! They were grilling me for twenty minutes about all sorts of shite. Eventually they believed I had nothing to do with Mi5 the CIA, the Mossad or any other network of creepers.

I arrived back into Nassau in the afternoon. I still had to wangle a flight back to the UK so I called the office in

Miami. "But we've already issued with a ticket? Where are you?" asked one of the girls in the office. "Erm...Nassau," I said. "Nassau? How on earth did you get there?" Anyway after a promise to drop her in some flowers and chocolates when I returned to the ship she thankfully issued tickets from the Bahamas to London the next day. Problem was, I only had a hundred bucks and needed somewhere to stay for the night in Nassau. I called jungle woman's mom and she came and picked me up from the airport. "Where have you just come from? The ship isn't in port and you're here at the airport?" She asked. "You don't want to know. But thanks for picking me up." I stayed at the ex's sisters house for the night so the jungle woman never knew I was in town.

A day later I was back in blighty doing a spot of sofa surfing again, and since I was back for only a few weeks it wasn't really much of an issue. I had a great time considering the circumstances and before I knew it, I was back on the jumbo jet sitting all the way back in steerage. No such luck trying to wangle my way into business class this time. Several hours later, I was back in Miami waiting for another flight for the Bahamas to rejoin the Majesty. The ship was having a refit whilst in Freeport.

I was happy to be back, not because I had any allegiance to the Majesty, but because it docked in the Bahamas for a few days a week. This did not last too long though; it must have been my unlucky year, because three weeks later I was dismissed for disorderly conduct. I won't really go into too much detail about the episode, however, I will tell you in no uncertain terms what actually happened.

SEVEN OUT

I got my ass fired after less than one month's service on the Majesty. This was supposedly going to be my third contract working upon her, but it wasn't to be. I had threatened to chin the captain of the Majesty of the Seas at a disciplinary meeting. This episode came around because the previous night I had thrown a picture I had bought over the side. "Why did you throw that picture over the side," asked the staff captain at the hearing. I did not know, and couldn't give him a straight answer. All the officers in the room looked at each other, then one said, "Were you drinking?" I knew there was no escape and I would be getting the sack either way, "Yes, unfortunately it was my night off and I had one or ten too many," I replied. "So it's pointless sending you down the medical centre for a blood test?" said the staff captain.
I just nodded my head. All was going smoothly, I was calm, cool and collected until the fucking captain put his rather large oar in. "Were you dropping off cocaine for the drug runners in Miami?" he asked. I squinted, and looked at him in amazement. "Dropping off drugs for the cartel? Do I look like a fucking cocaine dealer? I will come around there and punch you in the face?"
Oops! Now a lot of my mates think this quite funny, but I

actually think its pretty fucking sad now I have re -read this book after a number of years. I am literally staggered I acted in such an irrational and irresponsible manner under the influence of the the dreaded booze and it will get worse.

So within 24hrs I would be back in England, but fortunately this time, I had a few grand in my pocket to sort out some emergency accommodation. This wouldn't last long, so I needed to get yet another fucking job. I called the joint I had left a few years previously, the Circus. I managed to speak with one of my old managers immediately, "Is that you Windmill? Where have you been for the last two-years? We closed for refurbishment and you disappeared," asked the manager.
"Well, let me tell you what happened. I was supposed to go across the channel to France, to purchase some fags and wine, but unfortunately I embarked the wrong vessel and ended up in St Thomas in the Caribbean," I replied.
"Bollocks, you have been moonlighting and working for RCCL more like," replied the voice on the phone.
"You should never let the truth get between you and a good story," I retorted and everything was cool again.
"Fucking hell," I thought to myself, "you've let Sooty down by resigning off one of his ships for being wankered and now you've let your own sons' down repeating the same mistakes to end up in a shit casino you're going to hate?" Booze definitely distorted my mind and now I was somewhat focused again, the grave error of

previous judgement came home to fucking well roost. The option, given the circumstances was to hide the negativity and look for the positives.

Therefore, the only real bonus about returning to this club, was the fact they were supposedly putting a dice table in the casino. The place was not exactly what I thought it would be on my first shift. Nothing had really changed at all within the casino, in fact after spending over £1 million pounds on a refurbishment, the place looked considerably worse. Work that one out? The same old faces were still knocking about and the atmosphere in the pit wasn't great. The management team asked me if I would be interested in starting a trainee pit boss course. Initially I accepted, because I needed to stop fucking about and get a bit more serious about life. However, it did not take me long to get pissed off with the joint yet again because of the moody atmosphere and negative vibes surrounding the place. Therefore I gradually stopped turning up for my shifts, I was back on the dreaded lash once again. There is always an excuse. My gosh, I am beginning to sound like an old record with the needle stuck in a groove in the vinyl. Just repeating the same old verse without actually doing anything to change. If I was for once in my life be honest, and admit the booze seemed more appealing than the work, we might actually start to get somewhere.

My superstar mate Dorell would be on the phone for hours, day after day trying to coax me out of this dilemma. When I finally arose from my slumber, I would occasionally go across to visit her, to make sure she was OK. She had a great idea about us writing a book together, and we could later clash our lifestyles together in a novel. It was a good idea, because we'd both lived slightly on the wild side. Ms Maximus - as I liked to call her, always made me smile with her infectious personality and vibrant outlook on life.

"So, Pedro, what you going to do," said she.

"What about work? Fuck knows, probably the same as usual," I replied.

"No, I mean what are you going to do about taking me down to our favourite hangout Raphael's in Paradise Circus on Thursday? It's been ages since we've been down there, and you, you fucker owe me a good night out," she answered smiling. "Anyway, we have a lot to discuss, well you do, because you're going to come up with a good idea to make *me* some money!"

"Ha, ha fuck off, you're the one writing matey, I'm the director," I retorted.

"Well I'll tell you what sunshine, how about we meet up and talk about it, and then go to that fabulous restaurant next door for our favourite food, and it is on me," she replied smiling. Dorell makes me laugh, she really is an inspiration. Some of her stories and the way she managed to turn negatives into positives were superb. There wasn't too much in life that pissed her off, unless it was needless bullshit. Rome sprang to mind again, because those silly

Romans who treated her so appallingly had no idea of what a fantastic girl she really was. There loss, anyway, that is all in the past now and what is going on here is more important.

"OK matey you have a deal! One shall be in touch within the next few days, try and stay out of trouble until such time," I said. And with that, I left with a happy heart.

My old mate Shah needed a job, so I managed to get him a job at the Circus. Within weeks, I realized that I was not going to make the course; my head was somewhere else. I told the GM that I would not be continuing with the pit boss job. He asked me if I knew anybody who might be interested, I called Shah, and he came in that night and took over my roll. Several weeks later I managed to get fired from the Circus for instructing a trainee dealer to pay out a bet which was too much. Now, the booze was affecting my mind and work. After 25yrs in the casino industry I had never made such a mistake and now, the final curtain descended upon a once sparkling career. They suspended me whilst they conducted an internal enquiry into the issue, I was on gardening leave. I already knew the outcome, I was in an impossible position. For the three week suspension I sort of disappeared of the social radar, and sank into the depths of self inflicted despair.

Dorell, bless her, never let up once. She knew drinking was the problem; in fact she'd been in touch with my mom who told her that I'd basically scarified all my old friends for the bottle. That is the end game with excessive drinking, you become selfish and introverted. Instead of facing reality and finding a logical answer to any underlying issues, you hit the bottle and reality suddenly becomes fiction. The blame game is the easiest option; it is everybody else's fault for your troubles. The people you care about the most become the victims of your lunacy. You stop taking their calls, you ignore the messages and shrink into your own little world. Dorell had become cheesed off with me one week because I refused to talk, she knew I was on the lash and bombarded my phone with calls. Eventually I lifted the receiver and slurred "piss off I'm busy." Not too nice, but yet again, she refused to let up. She was constantly on me like a ton of bricks, and was ecstatic when finally I went over to see her a weeks later. I had brought her son some canvas so that he could get involved with art.

"Yo Windmill, you are looking superb my son," she said. "Hi ya darling, I am on my way to Upper Arley, but like I promised, I have brought some stuff for you and Louie the first," I replied.
"Have you started writing yet? I bet you haven't given it a thought," she asked.
"Mate, you know me better than I do," I replied smiling.
"Well I have started, so you'd better get it together later when you get home, or else! And you're right I do know you better than you do," she added laughing.
"Okay, calm down, I'll start latter tonight, I promise," I

answered. We gave each other a hug because it was great to see her again, she was like a sister. We had seen a lot together, the good the bad and the bewildering!

"Mate I am in a cab, so I must go, I will call you later matey," I told her.

"OK, thanks Windmill, we will definitely talk later OK?"

"Always mate," I replied.

A good thing started to happen around this time, I had taken an interest in programming computers, and I was fascinated how a simple set of instructions to a machine could make it perform complex operations. The web had become prevalent over the last decade, its power to communicate across the entire globe was, and still is astonishing. Therefore, I hit the library, and picked up some books on the subject. Within a few weeks I had managed to write some HTML to display basic web-page's; however, I had not yet secured any domain names, or set up any accounts with a server to make them live. The original building blocks of HTML were tables to display the text. It was in effect a tedious way to display information; however, a revolutionary concept had been making its presence felt in the web designing world called CSS - cascading style sheets, which gave the developer more control on the way pages could be displayed. Furthermore, an even more powerful aspect to web development began to make web-page's literally come alive. JavaScript is a language that executes on the browser and gives the page developer the chance to make their pages interactive with the user. Strictly speaking, HTML is not a programming language; it is just tags you fill with blocks information. Therefore, it is limited to what it can achieve. Instead of having the usual static page, you could now have images fading in and out of each other, and messages fly across the screen. It was going to be a lot to learn; however, I certainly was enjoying the prospect of starting a business, which incorporated the World Wide Web. My brother had been running a music business for a few years, and he sold t-shirts too. Since I had a long-standing interest in art, he suggested I make some designs via my computer that could be then reproduced via a machine. But first I had to learn all the relevant vector programs to make this a reality, and that was not going to happen overnight; however, it was definitely food for thought.

It was now Saturday afternoon, I had better call Dorell, I thought. I called the house to see how her trip to Scotland went; I got the shock of my life, "She's in hospital Windmill," said her daughter. For the fleeting second the words I had just heard did not register, and then my mind suddenly focused.
"What, what do you mean she is in hospital? What the fuck has happened,' I asked in shock.
"She collapsed at work; she is in critical condition in Selly Oak," answered Kiesha.
I literally dropped the phone in utter disbelief, I was thunderstruck; I could hardly believe what I had just

heard. I rushed down there, my mind was racing, I did not know what to think, or how serious her condition really was. My heart sank when I finally found her though; she looked terrible. Her father was by her bedside, he too looked extremely distraught by his daughters' appearance. I immediately knew that this was indeed very serious, she was barely conscious and, she had several different tubes thrust into her head and mouth.

"Dorell, mate, it is windmill," I said into her ear. I was struggling to hold in my emotions and I could feel my eyes welling up. "Mate, please, what has happened?" She did not say a word, but she recognized my voice instantaneously; she lifted her hand so that I could hold it. I did not even notice the huge boxing like gloves they had slipped over her hands. These had been firmly secured to her hands to stop her from ripping the tubes from her head and nose. She had suffered a brain haemorrhage at work, she had also fell and hit her head, which had caused her to have a fit. She had not gone to Scotland, because she felt she would have been too tired. This was the first time I had actually met her father and it definitely was not a good thing to speak with him under these circumstances. I eventually left the hospital in total shock.

The next day I returned and Dorell's condition had in fact deteriorated further, she had been on the operating table twice, and now things were suddenly looking extremely grim. The surgeon whom had operated on her called me and her dad to a private room, he then sadly informed her father and me that Dorell would not be the same again. He summarized and said she had suffered a shortage of oxygen to the brain, and that she would be brain damaged, I felt pummelled. Both of us offered the surgeon any parts of our bodies in desperation to help, as if by magic he could take parts of us to fix her. This is how utterly stunned and desperate we were to try and keep Dorell alive. But it was to no avail. I had previously spoken to Kiesha prior to the hospital visit and told her I would pop in to see her after the visit, she only lived literally ten minutes away down the road; and in stunned silence, that is exactly where I headed

I arrived at her flat in Harbourne and gained my composure before ringing the intercom. One of Dorell's cousins' answered, and she immediately buzzed me to enter. I did not really want to be here under such terrible circumstances, but I promised Kiesha that I would visit to leave her some monies for school to try and help out whilst her mom was in hospital. I spoke briefly with Dorell's aunties and cousins, and then I went to speak to Kiesha. Kiesha knew immediately that something had gone terribly wrong; the initial look of happiness to see me was immediately replaced by a look of concern. I did not have to say a word because the look on my face said it all.

"You are very upset aren't you, what has happened?" asked Kiesha. She already knew the doctors had drilled her skull, trying to relieve the pressure on her brain. Tears were forming in her eyes and for once in my life I was totally lost for words. All I could do was try and comfort her, she was just a kid really and she had nobody else apart from her mother. We continued to talk for a while and then the time came for me to leave. We hugged each other and I told I would be in touch the very next day. It was heartbreaking to see her cry, and I refused to tell her the extent of the problems awaiting Dorell, but I knew deep inside that she already knew what was going to happen. The next day I went down to the hospital and a sincere sadness descended over me, I had such a terrible feeling now, things were becoming desperate. I spoke in her ear, I told her that I loved her like a sister but it was apparent she was in serious trouble now; it was just a waiting game, circumstances were out of anybody's control.

That evening her father called and told me the devastating news. Dorell was brain dead and he'd already made the difficult decision to turn off her life support machine the next day under the instruction of the doctors. They had explained to him that there was little point in keeping her alive because she'd never be able to walk or talk ever again. He asked me if I wanted to be at her bedside. I told him that I could not bear to see her in death, it was just too heartbreaking.

She died on the 15th of November 2008, at the tender age of thirty-five. A part of me died too that day, I lost a true friend. This was the day I forgot all about god. It did not really matter to me what any religious person said anymore; no words could sooth my utter disappointment, or absolute shock at her passing. Rest in Peace Dorell.

sic transit gloria mundi

LIFE AFTER CASINOS

Amazing how so many things can happen in such a short amount of time, the triumphs and the tragedies. I think quite a bit about some of the extraordinary people I have been fortunate to meet whilst on my international travels in the casino industry. So many of the old brigade have sadly, passed on now. However, casino staffs are actually like a family and many of us still stay in touch with each other regardless of where we are in the world today.

I actually learnt to code computers since leaving the casino industry, and set up a Private Limited Company. Even opening a shop that revolved around printing, which was driven by the websites I had actually built myself. This in itself, to me, was a tremendously proud moment, simply because I had taught myself something of which I had a profound interest. Being back in Birmingham has been difficult in so many ways because in reality, I have found hard to readjust to normal living.

Do I miss the casino business? Of course, I have been out for over 7yrs now – *seven out* :) however, it would be impossible to replicate the days gone by, or live that life in the industry today. Nothing ever remains the same, and I can thank my lucky stars I had the chance to be paid to work all over the world in a job, which was incredibly satisfying. There are very few chances for people to be offered all expenses paid positions in various exotic locations in the world. This is what the casino industry used to be, this is what I loved, and is something that changed my life forever.

THE END

Acknowledgements

Big thank you to all the casinos and sailors world wide for some pretty amazing times on the high seas. Also, to the people in Florida for teaching me to sail. Further, I would like to mention all the fantastic pubs, bars and clubs I've been fortunate to visit in many exotic locations around the world.

Notes

So, now this little story – with its appalling grammar and poorly structured layout has finally come to an end, I have realized the majority of the book makes me look like a dickhead! I couldn't fill a book full of boring poncy shite which goes onboard ships, so opted for the wild side on the high seas. Most casino staff are normal, well a good percentage of them are, and my exploits are not a reflection on all casino staff in general.

For those interested in further readings, I have also a serious fictional crime thriller set in the 1900s called the Return of the Revenge. You can copy and paste the link to short story below.

Ebook:

http://www.lulu.com/shop/http://www.lulu.com/shop/peter-smith/return-of-the-revenge/ebook/product-22597866.html

Paperback:

http://www.lulu.com/shop/http://www.lulu.com/shop/peter-smith/return-of-the-revenge/paperback/product-22597870.html

If you're interested in farce, I have also published a book called Tales from the Telegraph, which basically rips the shit out of lefties.

Ebook:

http://www.lulu.com/shop/peter-smith/tales-from-the-telegraph/ebook/product-22577853.html

Paperback:

http://www.lulu.com/shop/http://www.lulu.com/shop/peter-smith/tales-from-the-telegraph/paperback/product-22577371.html

Best wishes, Windmill MMXVI.

Printed in Dunstable, United Kingdom